MELCHIOR'S DREAM

AND OTHER TALES

JULIANA HORATIA EWING

1st WORLD
LIBRARY
Literary Society

Melchior's Dream and Other Tales

Juliana Horatia Ewing

© 1st World Library, 2007
PO Box 2211
Fairfield, IA 52556
www.1stworldlibrary.com
First Edition

LCCN: 2007932069

Softcover ISBN: 978-1-4218-4846-4
Hardcover ISBN: 978-1-4218-4749-8
eBook ISBN: 978-1-4218-4943-0

Purchase *"Melchior's Dream and Other Tales"*
as a traditional bound book at:
www.1stWorldLibrary.com/purchase.asp?ISBN=978-1-4218-4846-4

1st World Library is a literary, educational organization
dedicated to:

- Creating a free internet library of downloadable ebooks

- Hosting writing competitions and offering book publishing
  scholarships.

1st World Library Literary Society

Giving Back to the World

"If you want to work on the core problem, it's early school literacy."

- James Barksdale, former CEO of Netscape

"No skill is more crucial to the future of a child, or to a democratic and prosperous society, than literacy."

- Los Angeles Times

"Literacy... means far more than learning how to read and write... The aim is to transmit... knowledge and promote social participation."

- UNESCO

"Literacy is not a luxury, it is a right and a responsibility. If our world is to meet the challenges of the twenty-first century we must harness the energy and creativity of all our citizens."

- President Bill Clinton

"Parents should be encouraged to read to their children, and teachers should be equipped with all available techniques for teaching literacy, so the varying needs and capacities of individual kids can be taken into account."

- Hugh Mackay

Dedicated

TO

FOUR BROTHERS AND FOUR SISTERS

CONTENTS

EDITOR'S PREFACE

It is always a memorable era in a mother's life when she first introduces a daughter into society. Many things contribute to make it so; among which is the fact of the personal blessing to herself, in having been permitted to see the day—to have been spared, that is, to watch over her child in infancy, and now to see her entering life upon her own account.

But a more uncommon privilege is the one granted to me on the present occasion, of introducing a daughter into the literary world; and the feelings of pride and pleasure it calls forth, are certainly not less powerful than those created by the commoner occurrence. It is my comfort also to add that these are not overclouded by any painful anxiety or misgiving. There may be differences of opinion as to the precise amount of literary merit in these tales; but viewed as the first productions of a young author, they are surely full of promise; while their whole tone and aim is so unmistakably high, that even those who criticize the style will be apt to respect the writer.

I ought here to express a hope that it will not be thought presumptuous on my part, to undertake the office of introduction. I beg it to be understood that I address myself especially to those readers who have (I speak it with deep gratitude and pleasure) listened kindly and favourably to me for several years past, and who will, I trust, be no less well disposed towards my daughter's writings.

To them also it may be interesting to know, that in the "J.H.G." of "Melchior's Dream," etc., they will find the original of my own portrait of "Aunt Judy."

But I have still something more to say: another little bit of gratification to express. What one sister has written, another has illustrated by her pencil; a cause of double thankfulness in my heart to Him from whom all good gifts come.

MARGARET GATTY.

NOTE.—*The foregoing Preface was written for the first edition of "Melchior's Dream, and other Tales." This was published in 1862 under Mrs. Ewing's maiden initials, "J.H.G." It contained the first five stories in the present volume, and these were illustrated by the writer's eldest sister, "M.S.G."*

MELCHIOR'S DREAM

AN ALLEGORY.

"Thou that hast given so much to me, Give one thing more—a grateful heart."

—GEORGE HERBERT

"Well, father, I don't believe the Browns are a bit better off than we are; and yet when I spent the day with young Brown, we cooked all sorts of messes in the afternoon; and he wasted twice as much rum and brandy and lemons in his trash, as I should want to make good punch of. He was quite surprised, too, when I told him that our mince-pies were kept shut up in the larder, and only brought out at meal-times, and then just one apiece; he said they had mince-pies always going, and he got one whenever he liked. Old Brown never blows up about that sort of thing; he likes Adolphus to enjoy himself in the holidays, particularly at Christmas."

The speaker was a boy—if I may be allowed to use the word in speaking of an individual whose jackets had for some time past been resigned to a younger member of his family, and who daily, in the privacy of his own apartment, examined his soft cheeks by the aid of his sisters' "back-hair glass." He was a handsome boy too; tall, and like David—"ruddy, and of a fair countenance;" and his face, though clouded then, bore the expression of general amiability. He was the eldest son in a large young family, and was being educated at one of the best public schools. He did not, it must be confessed, think either small beer or small beans of himself; and as to the beer and beans that his family thought of him, I think it was pale ale and kidney-beans at least.

Young Hopeful had, however, his weak points like the rest of us; and perhaps one of the weakest was the difficulty he found in amusing himself without *bothering* other people. He had quite a monomania for proposing the most troublesome "larks" at the most inconvenient moments; and if his plans were thwarted, an AEolian harp is cheerful compared to the tone in which, arguing and lamenting, he

"Fought his battles o'er again,"

to the distraction of every occupied member of the household.

When the lords of the creation of all ages can find nothing else to do, they generally take to eating and drinking; and so it came to pass that our hero had set his mind upon brewing a jorum of punch, and sipping it with an accompaniment of mince-pies; and Paterfamilias had not been quietly settled to his writing for half-an-hour, when he was disturbed by an application for the necessary ingredients. These he had refused, quietly explaining that he could not afford to waste his French brandy, etc., in school-boy cookery, and ending with, "You see the reason, my dear boy?"

To which the dear boy replied as above, and concluded with the disrespectful (not to say ungrateful) hint, "Old Brown never blows up about that sort of thing; he likes Adolphus to enjoy himself in the holidays."

Whereupon Paterfamilias made answer, in the mildly depre-cating tone in which the elder sometimes do answer the younger in these topsy-turvy days:—

"That's quite a different case. Don't you see, my boy, that Adolphus Brown is an only son, and you have nine brothers and sisters? If you have punch and mince-meat to play with, there is no reason why Tom should not have it, and James, and Edward, and William, and Benjamin, and Jack. And then there are your sisters. Twice the amount of the Browns' mince-meat would not serve you. I like you to enjoy yourself in the holidays as much as young Brown or anybody; but you must remember that I send you boys to good schools, and give you all the substantial comforts and advantages in my power; and the Christmas bills are very heavy, and I have a great many calls on my purse; and you must be reasonable. Don't you see?"

"Well, father—" began the boy; but his father interrupted him. He knew the unvarying beginning of a long grumble, and dreading the argument, cut it short.

"I have decided. You must amuse yourself some other way. And just remember that young Brown's is quite another case. He is an only son."

Whereupon Paterfamilias went off to his study and his sermon; and his son, like the Princess in Andersen's story of the Swineherd, was left outside to sing,

"O dearest Augustine,
All's clean gone away!"

Not that he did say that—that was the princess' song—what

he said was,

"*I wish I were an only son!*"

This was rather a vain wish, for round the dining-room fire (where he soon joined them) were gathered his nine brothers and sisters, who, to say the truth, were not looking much more lively and cheerful than he. And yet (of all days in the year on which to be doleful and dissatisfied!) this was Christmas Eve.

Now I know that the idea of dulness or discomfort at Christmas is a very improper one, particularly in a story. We all know how every little boy in a story-book spends the Christmas holidays.

First, there is the large hamper of good things sent by grand-papa, which is as inexhaustible as Fortunatus's purse, and contains everything, from a Norfolk turkey to grapes from the grandpaternal vinery.

There is the friend who gives a guinea to each member of the family, and sees who will spend it best.

There are the godpapas and godmammas, who might almost be fairy sponsors from the number of expensive gifts that they bring upon the scene. The uncles and aunts are also liberal.

One night is devoted to a magic-lantern (which has a perfect focus), another to the pantomime, a third to a celebrated conjuror, a fourth to a Christmas tree and juvenile ball.

The happy youth makes himself sufficiently ill with plum-pudding, to testify to the reader how good it was, and how much there was of it; but recovers in time to fall a victim to the negus and trifle at supper for the same reason. He is neither fatigued with late hours nor surfeited with sweets; or if he is, we do not hear of it.

But as this is a strictly candid history, I will at once confess the truth, on behalf of my hero and his brothers and sisters. They had spent the morning in decorating the old church, in pricking holly about the house, and in making a mistletoe bush. Then in the afternoon they had tasted the Christmas soup and seen it given out; they had put a finishing touch to the snow man by crowning him with holly, and had dragged the yule-logs home from the carpenter's. And now, the early tea being over, Paterfamilias had gone to finish his sermon for to-morrow; his friend was shut up in his room; and Materfamilias was in hers, with one of those painful headaches which even Christmas will not always keep away. So the ten children were left to amuse themselves, and they found it rather a difficult matter.

"Here's a nice Christmas!" said our hero. He had turned his youngest brother out of the arm-chair, and was now lying in it with his legs over the side. "Here's a nice Christmas! A fellow might just as well be at school. I wonder what Adolphus Brown would think of being cooped up with a lot of children like this! It's his party to-night, and he's to have champagne and ices. I wish I were an only son."

"Thank you," said a chorus of voices from the floor. They were all sprawling about on the hearth-rug, pushing and struggling like so many kittens in a sack, and every now and then with a grumbled remonstrance:—

"Don't, Jack! you're treading on me."

"You needn't take all the fire, Tom."

"Keep your legs to yourself, Benjamin."

"It wasn't I," etc., with occasionally the feebler cry of a small sister—

"Oh! you boys are so rough."

"And what are you girls, I wonder?" inquired the proprietor of the arm-chair with cutting irony. "Whiney piney, whiney piney. I wish there were no such things as brothers and sisters!"

"*You wish* WHAT?" said a voice from the shadow by the door, as deep and impressive as that of the ghost in Hamlet.

The ten sprang up; but when the figure came into the fire-light, they saw that it was no ghost, but Paterfamilias's old college friend, who spent most of his time abroad, and who, having no home or relatives of his own, had come to spend Christmas at his friend's vicarage. "You wish *what*?" he repeated.

"Well, brothers and sisters are a bore," was the reply. "One or two would be all very well; but just look, here are ten of us; and it just spoils everything. If a fellow wants to go anywhere, it's somebody else's *turn*. If old Brown sends a basket of grapes, it's share and share alike; all the ten must taste, and then there's about a grape and a half for each. If anybody calls or comes to luncheon, there are a whole lot of brats swarming about, looking as if we kept a school. Whatever one does, the rest must do; whatever there is, the rest must share; whereas, if a fellow was an only son, he would have the whole—and by all the rules of arithmetic, one is better than a tenth."

"And by the same rules ten is better than one," said the friend.

Juliana Horatia Ewing

"Sold again," sang out Master Jack from the floor, and went head over heels against the fender.

His brother boxed his ears with great promptitude, and went on, "Well, I don't care; confess, sir, isn't it rather a nuisance?"

Paterfamilias's friend looked very grave, and said, quietly, "I don't think I am able to judge. I never had brother or sister but one, and he was drowned at sea. Whatever I have had, I have had the whole of, and would have given it away willingly for some one to give it to. If any one sent me grapes, I ate them alone. If I made anything, there was no one to show it to. If I wanted to act, I must act all the characters, and be my own audience. I remember that I got a lot of sticks at last, and cut heads and faces to all of them, and carved names on their sides, and called them my brothers and sisters. If you want to know what I thought a nice number for a fellow to have, I can only say that I remember carving twenty-five. I used to stick them in the ground and talk to them. I have been only, and lonely, and alone, all my life, and have never felt the nuisance you speak of."

This was a funny account; but the speaker looked so far from funny that one of the sisters, who was very tender-hearted, crept up to him, and said, gently—

"Richard is only joking; he doesn't really want to get rid of us. The other day the curate said he wished he had a sister, and Richard offered to sell us all for ninepence; but he is only in fun. Only it is rather slow just now, and the boys get rather cross; at least, we all of us do."

"It's a dreadful state of things," said the friend, smiling through his black beard and moustachios. "What is to be done?"

"I know what would be very nice," insinuated the young lady.

"What?"

"If you wouldn't mind telling us a very short story till supper-time. The boys like stories."

"That's a good idea," said Benjamin. "As if the girls didn't!"

But the friend proclaimed order, and seated himself with the girl in question on his knee. "Well, what sort of a story is it to be?"

"Any sort," said Richard; "only not too true, if you please. I don't like stories like tracts. There was an usher at a school I was at, and he used to read tracts about good boys and bad boys to the fellows on Sunday afternoon. He always took out the real names, and put in the names of the fellows instead. Those who had done well in the week he put in as good ones, and those who hadn't as the bad. He didn't like me, and I was always put in as a bad boy, and I came to so many untimely ends I got sick of it. I was hanged twice, and transported once for sheep-stealing; I committed suicide one week, and broke into the bank the next; I ruined three families, became a hopeless drunkard, and broke the hearts of my twelve distinct parents. I used to beg him to let me be reformed next week; but he said he never would till I did my Caesar better. So, if you please, we'll have a story that can't be true."

"Very well," said the friend, laughing; "but if it isn't true, may I put you in? All the best writers, you know, draw their characters from their friends now-a-days. May I put you in?"

"Oh, certainly!" said Richard, placing himself in front of the fire, putting his feet on the hob, and stroking his curls with an air which seemed to imply that whatever he was put into would be highly favoured.

The rest struggled, and pushed, and squeezed themselves into more modest but equally comfortable quarters; and after a few moments of thought, Paterfamilias's friend commenced the story of

MELCHIOR'S DREAM.

"Melchior is my hero. He was—well, he considered himself a young man, so we will consider him so too. He was not perfect; but in these days the taste in heroes is for a good deal of imperfection, not to say wickedness. He was not an only son. On the contrary, he had a great many brothers and sisters, and found them quite as objectionable as my friend Richard does."

"I smell a moral," murmured the said Richard.

"Your scent must be keen," said the story-teller, "for it is a long way off. Well, he had never felt them so objectionable as on one particular night, when, the house being full of company, it was decided that the boys should sleep in 'barracks,' as they called it; that is, all in one large room."

"Thank goodness, we have not come to that!" said the incorrigible Richard; but he was reduced to order by threats of being turned out, and contented himself with burning the soles of his boots against the bars of the grate in silence: and the friend continued:—

"But this was not the worst. Not only was he, Melchior, to sleep in the same room with his brothers, but his bed being the longest and largest, his youngest brother was to sleep at the other end of it—foot to foot. True, by this means he got another pillow, for, of course, that little Hop-o'-my-Thumb could do without one, and so he took his; but, in spite of this, he determined that, sooner than submit to such an indignity, he would sit up all night. Accordingly, when all the rest were fast asleep, Melchior, with his boots off and his waistcoat easily unbuttoned, sat over the fire in the long lumber-room which served that night as 'barracks'. He had refused to eat any supper downstairs to mark his displeasure, and now repaid himself by a stolen meal according to his own taste. He had got a pork-pie, a little bread and cheese, some large onions to roast, a couple of raw apples, an orange, and papers of soda and tartaric acid to compound effervescing draughts. When these dainties were finished, he proceeded to warm some beer in a pan, with ginger, spice, and sugar, and then lay back in his chair and sipped it slowly, gazing before him, and thinking over his misfortunes.

"The night wore on, the fire got lower and lower, and still Melchior sat, with his eyes fixed on a dirty old print that had hung above the mantelpiece for years, sipping his 'brew', which was fast getting cold. The print represented an old man in a light costume, with a scythe in one hand and an hour-glass in the other; and underneath the picture in flourishing capitals was the word TIME.

"'You're a nice old beggar,' said Melchior, dreamily. 'You look like an old hay-maker who has come to work in his shirt-sleeves, and forgotten the rest of his clothes. Time! time you went to the tailor's, I think.'"

"This was very irreverent; but Melchior was not in a respectful mood; and as for the old man, he was as calm as any philosopher."

"The night wore on, and the fire got lower and lower, and at last went out altogether."

"'How stupid of me not to have mended it!' said Melchior; but he had not mended it, and so there was nothing for it but to go to bed; and to bed he went accordingly."

"'But I won't go to sleep,' he said; 'no, no; I shall keep awake, and to-morrow they shall know that I have had a bad night.'"

"So he lay in bed with his eyes wide open, and staring still at the old print, which he could see from his bed by the light of the candle, which he had left alight on the mantelpiece to keep him awake. The flame waved up and down, for the room was draughty; and as the lights and shadows passed over the old man's face, Melchior almost fancied that it nodded to him, so he nodded back again; and as that tired him he shut his eyes for a few seconds. When he opened them again, there was no longer any doubt—the old man's head was moving; and not only his head, but his legs, and his whole body. Finally, he put his feet out of the frame, and prepared to step right over the mantelpiece, candle, and all.

"'Take care,' Melchior tried to say, 'you'll set fire to your shirt.' But he could not utter a sound; and the old man arrived safely on the floor, where he seemed to grow larger and larger, till he was fully the size of a man, but still with the same scythe and hour-glass, and the same airy costume. Then he came across the room, and sat down by Melchior's bedside.

"'Who are you?' said Melchior, feeling rather creepy."

"'TIME,' said his visitor in a deep voice, which sounded as if it came from a distance."

"'Oh, to be sure, yes! In copper-plate capitals.'"

"'What's in copper-plate capitals?' inquired Time."

"'Your name, under the print.'"

"'Very likely,' said Time."

"Melchior felt more and more uneasy. 'You must be very cold,' he said. 'Perhaps you would feel warmer if you went back into the picture.'

"'Not at all,' said Time; 'I have come on purpose to see you.'"

"'I have not the pleasure of knowing you,' said Melchior, trying to keep his teeth from chattering."

"'There are not many people who have a personal acquaintance with me,' said his visitor. 'You have an advantage—I am your godfather.'

"'Indeed,' said Melchior; 'I never heard of it.'"

"'Yes,' said his visitor; 'and you will find it a great advantage.'"

"'Would you like to put on my coat?' said Melchior, trying to be civil."

"'No, thank you,' was the answer. 'You will want it yourself. We must be driving soon.'

"'Driving!' said Melchior."

"'Yes,' was the answer; 'all the world is driving; and you must drive; and here come your brothers and sisters.'"

Juliana Horatia Ewing

"Melchior sat up; and there they were, sure enough, all dressed, and climbing one after the other on to the bed—*his* bed!

"There was that little minx of a sister with her curls (he always called them carrot shavings), who was so conceited (girls always are!) and always trying to attract notice, in spite of Melchior's incessant snubbings. There was that clever brother, with his untidy hair and bent shoulders, who was just as bad the other way; who always ran out of the back door when visitors called, and was for ever moping and reading: and this, in spite of Melchior's hiding his books, and continually telling him that he was a disgrace to the family, a perfect bear, not fit to be seen, etc.—all with the laudable desire of his improvement. There was that little Hop-o'-my-Thumb, as lively as any of them, a young monkey, the worst of all; who was always in mischief, and consorting with the low boys in the village; though Melchior did not fail to tell him that he was not fit company for gentlemen's sons, that he was certain to be cut when he went to school, and that he would probably end his days by being transported, if not hanged. There was the second brother, who was Melchior's chief companion, and against whom he had no particular quarrel. And there was the little pale lame sister, whom he dearly loved; but whom, odd to say, he never tried to improve at all; his remedy for her failings was generally, 'Let her do as she likes, will you?' There were others who were all tiresome in their respective ways; and one after the other they climbed up.

"'What are you doing, getting on to my bed!' inquired the indignant brother, as soon as he could speak."

"'Don't you know the difference between a bed and a coach, godson?' said Time, sharply."

"Melchior was about to retort, but on looking round, he saw that they were really in a large sort of coach with very wide windows. 'I thought I was in bed,' he muttered. 'What can I have been dreaming of?'

"'What, indeed!' said the godfather. 'But, be quick, and sit close, for you have all to get in; you are all brothers and sisters.'"

"'Must families be together?' inquired Melchior, dolefully."

"'Yes, at first,' was the answer; 'they get separated in time. In fact, everyone has to cease driving sooner or later. I drop them on the road at different stages, according to my orders,' and he showed a bundle of papers in his hands; 'but, as I favour you, I will tell you in confidence that I have to drop all your brothers and sisters before you. There, you four oldest sit on this side, you five others there, and the little one must stand or be nursed.'"

"'Ugh!' said Melchior, 'the coach would be well enough if one was alone; but what a squeeze with all these brats! I say, go pretty quick, will you?'"

"'I will,' said Time, 'if you wish it. But, beware that you cannot change your mind. If I go quicker for your sake, I shall never go slow again; if slower, I shall not again go quick; and I only favour you so far, because you are my godson. Here, take the check-string; when you want me, pull it, and speak through the tube. Now we're off.'"

"Whereupon the old man mounted the box, and took the reins. He had no whip; but when he wanted to start, he shook the hour-glass, and off they went. Then Melchior saw that the road where they were driving was very broad, and so filled with vehicles of all kinds that he could not see the hedges. The noise and crowd and dust were very great; and to Melchior all seemed delightfully exciting. There was every sort of conveyance, from the grandest coach to the humblest donkey-cart; and they seemed to have enough to do to escape being run over. Among all the gay people there were many whom he knew; and a very nice thing it seemed to be to drive among all the grandees, and to show his handsome face at the window, and bow and smile to his acquaintance. Then it appeared to be the fashion to wrap oneself in a tiger-skin rug, and to look at life through an opera-glass, and old Time had kindly put one of each into the coach.

"But here again Melchior was much troubled by his brothers and sisters. Just at the moment when he was wishing to look most fashionable and elegant, one or other of them would pull away the rug, or drop the glass, or quarrel, or romp, or do something that spoilt the effect. In fact, one and all, they 'just spoilt everything;' and the more he scolded, the worse they became. The 'minx' shook her curls, and flirted through the window with a handsome but ill-tempered looking man on a fine horse, who praised her 'golden locks,' as he called them; and, oddly enough, when Melchior said the man was a lout, and that the locks in question were corkscrewy carrot shavings, she only seemed to like the man and his compliments the more. Meanwhile, the untidy brother pored over his book, or if he came to the window, it was only to ridicule the fine ladies and gentlemen, so Melchior sent him to Coventry. Then Hop-o'-my-Thumb had taken to make signs and exchange jokes with some disreputable-looking youths in a dog-cart; and when his brother would have put him to 'sit still like a gentleman' at the bottom of the coach, he seemed positively to prefer his low companions; and the rest were little better.

"Poor Melchior! Surely there never was a clearer case of a

young gentleman's comfort destroyed, solely by other people's perverse determination to be happy in their own way instead of in his. Surely, no young gentleman ever knew better that if his brothers and sisters would yield to his wishes, they would not quarrel; or ever more completely overlooked the fact, that if he had yielded more to theirs the same happy result might have been attained. At last he lost patience, and pulling the check-string, bade Godfather Time drive as fast as he could.

"'For,' said he, 'there will never be any peace while there are so many of us in the coach; if a fellow had the rug and glass, and, indeed, the coach to himself, he might drive and bow and talk with the best of them; but as it is, one might as well go about in a wild-beast caravan.'"

"Godfather Time frowned, but shook his glass all the same, and away they went at a famous pace. All at once they came to a stop."

"'Now for it,' says Melchior; 'here goes one at any rate.'"

"Time called out the name of the second brother over his shoulder; and the boy stood up, and bade his brothers and sisters good-bye."

"'It is time that I began to push my way in the world,' said he, and passed out of the coach, and in among the crowd."

"'You have taken the only quiet boy,' said Melchior to the godfather angrily. 'Drive fast now, for pity's sake; and let us get rid of the tiresome ones.'"

"And fast enough they drove, and dropped first one and then the other; but the sisters, and the reading boy, and the youngest still remained."

"'What are you looking at?' said Melchior to the lame sister."

"'At a strange figure in the crowd,' she answered."

"'I see nothing,' said Melchior. But on looking again after a while, he did see a figure wrapped in a cloak, gliding in and out among the people, unnoticed, if not unseen."

"'Who is it?' Melchior asked of the godfather."

"'A friend of mine,' Time answered. 'His name is Death.'"

"Melchior shuddered, more especially as the figure had now come up to the coach, and put its hand in through the window, on which, to his horror, the lame sister laid hers and smiled. At this moment the coach stopped.

"'What are you doing?' shrieked Melchior, 'Drive on! drive on!'"

"But even while he sprang up to seize the check-string the door had opened, the pale sister's face (a little paler now) had dropped upon the shoulder of the figure in the cloak, and he had carried her away; and Melchior stormed and raved in vain.

"'To take her, and to leave the rest! Cruel! cruel!'"

"In his rage and grief, he hardly knew it when the untidy brother was called, and putting his book under his arm, slipped out of the coach without looking to the right or left. Presently the coach stopped again; and when Melchior looked up the door was open, and at it was the fine man on the fine horse, who was lifting the sister on to the saddle before him. 'What fool's game are you playing?' said Melchior, angrily. 'I know that man. He is both ill-tempered and a bad character.'"

"'You never told her so before,' muttered young Hop-o'-my-Thumb."

"'Hold your tongue,' said Melchior. 'I forbade her to talk to him, which was enough.'"

"'I don't want to leave you; but he cares for me, and you don't,' sobbed the sister; and she was carried away."

"When she had gone, the youngest brother slid down from his corner and came up to Melchior."

"'We are alone now, Brother,' he said; 'let us be good friends. May I sit on the front seat with you, and have half the rug? I will be very good and polite, and will have nothing more to do with those fellows, if you will talk to me.'"

"Now Melchior really rather liked the idea, but as his brother seemed to be in a submissive mood, he thought he would take the opportunity of giving him a good lecture, and would then graciously relent and forgive. So he began by asking him if he thought that he was fit company for him (Melchior), what he thought that gentlefolks would say to a boy who had been playing with such youths as young Hop-o'-my-Thumb had, and whether the said youths were not scoundrels? And when the boy refused to say that they were (for they had been kind to him), Melchior said that his tastes were evidently as bad as ever, and even hinted at the old transportation threat. This was too much; the boy went angrily back to his window corner, and Melchior—like too many of us!—lost the opportunity of making peace for the sake of wagging his own tongue.

"'But he will come round in a few minutes,' he thought A few minutes passed, however, and there was no sign. A few minutes more, and there was a noise, a shout; Melchior looked up, and saw that the boy had jumped through the open window into the road, and had been picked up by the men in the dog-cart, and was gone.

"And so at last my hero was alone. At first he enjoyed it very much. He shook out his hair, wrapped himself in the rug, stared through the opera-glass, and did the fine gentleman very well indeed. But though everyone allowed him to be the finest young fellow on the road, yet nobody seemed to care for the fact as much as he did; they talked, and complimented, and stared at him, but he got tired of it. For he could not arrange his hair any better; he could not dispose the rug more gracefully, or stare more perseveringly through the glass; and if he could, his friends could do nothing more than they had done. In fact, he got tired of the crowd, and found himself gazing through the window, not to see his fine friends, but to try and catch sight of his brothers and sisters. Sometimes he saw the youngest brother, looking each time more wild and reckless; and sometimes the sister, looking more and more miserable; but he saw no one else.

"At last there was a stir among the people, and all heads were turned towards the distance, as if looking for something. Melchior asked what it was, and was told that the people were looking for a man, the hero of many battles, who had won honour for himself and for his country in foreign lands, and who was coming home. Everybody stood up and gazed, Melchior with them. Then the crowd parted, and the hero came on. No one asked whether he were handsome or genteel, whether he kept good company, or wore a tiger-skin rug, or looked through an opera-glass? They knew what he had *done*, and it was enough.

"He was a bronzed hairy man, with one sleeve empty, and a

breast covered with stars; but in his face, brown with sun and wind, overgrown with hair and scarred with wounds, Melchior saw his second brother! There was no doubt of it. And the brother himself, though he bowed kindly in answer to the greetings showered on him, was gazing anxiously for the old coach, where he used to ride and be so uncomfortable, in that time to which he now looked back as the happiest of his life.

"'I thank you, gentlemen. I am indebted to you, gentlemen. I have been away long. I am going home.'"

"'Of course he is!' shouted Melchior, waving his arms widely with pride and joy. 'He is coming home; to this coach, where he was—oh, it seems but an hour ago! Time goes so fast. We were great friends when we were young together. My brother and I, ladies and gentlemen, the hero and I—my brother— the hero with the stars upon his breast—he is coming home!'"

"Alas! what avail stars and ribbons on a breast where the life-blood is trickling slowly from a little wound? The crowd looked anxious; the hero came on, but more slowly, with his dim eyes straining for the old coach; and Melchior stood with his arms held out in silent agony. But just when he was beginning to hope, and the brothers seemed about to meet, a figure passed between—a figure in a cloak.

"'I have seen you many times, Friend, face to face,' said the hero; 'but now I would fain have waited for a little while.'"

"'To enjoy his well-earned honours,' murmured the crowd."

"'Nay,' he said, 'not that; but to see my home, and my brothers and sisters. But if it may not be, friend Death, I am ready, and tired too.' With that he held out his hand, and Death lifted up the hero of many battles like a child, and carried him away, stars and ribbons and all.

"'Cruel Death!' cried Melchior; 'was there no one else in all this crowd, that you must take him?'"

"His friends condoled with him; but they soon went on their own ways; and the hero seemed to be forgotten; and Melchior, who had lost all pleasure in the old bowings and chattings, sat sadly gazing out of the window, to see if he could see any one for whom he cared. At last, in a grave dark man, who was sitting on a horse, and making a speech to the crowd, he recognized his clever untidy brother.

"'What is that man talking about?' he asked of some one near him."

"'That man!' was the answer. 'Don't you know? He is *the* man of the time. He is a philosopher. Everybody goes to hear him. He has found out that—well—that everything is a mistake.'"

"'Has he corrected it?' said Melchior."

"'You had better hear for yourself,' said the man. 'Listen.'"

"Melchior listened, and a cold clear voice rang upon his ear, saying:—

"'The world of fools will go on as they have ever done; but to the wise few, to whom I address myself, I would say—Shake off at once and for ever the fancies and feelings, the creeds and customs that shackle you, and be true. We have come to a time when wise men will not be led blindfold in the footsteps of their predecessors, but will tear away the bandage and see for themselves. I have torn away mine, and looked. There is no Faith—it is shaken to its rotten foundation; there is no Hope—it is disappointed every day; there is no Love at all. There is nothing for any man or for each, but his fate; and he is happiest and wisest who can meet it most unmoved."'

"'It is a lie!' shouted Melchior. 'I feel it to be so in my heart. A wicked foolish lie! Oh! was it to teach such evil folly as this that you left home and us, my brother? Oh, come back! come back!'"

"The philosopher turned his head coldly, and smiled. 'I thank the gentleman who spoke,' he said, still in the same cold voice, 'for his bad opinion, and for his good wishes. I think the gentleman spoke of home and kindred. My experience of life has led me to find that home is most valued when it is left, and kindred most dear when they are parted. I have happily freed myself from such inconsistencies. I am glad to know that fate can tear me from no place that I care for more than the next where it shall deposit me, nor take away any friends that I value more than those it leaves. I recommend a similar self-emancipation to the gentleman who did me the honour of speaking.'"

"With this the philosopher went his way, and the crowd followed him."

"'There is a separation more bitter than death,' said Melchior."

"At last he pulled the check-string, and called to Godfather Time in an humble entreating voice."

"'It is not your fault,' he began; 'it is not your fault, Godfather; but this drive has been altogether wrong. Let us turn back and begin again. Let us all get in afresh and begin again.'"

"'But what a squeeze with all the brats!' said Godfather Time, ironically."

"'We should be so happy,' murmured Melchior, humbly; 'and it is very cold and chilly; we should keep each other warm.'"

"'You have the tiger-skin rug and the opera-glass, you know,' said Time."

"'Ah, do not speak of me!' cried Melchior, earnestly. 'I am thinking of them. There is plenty of room; the little one can sit on my knee; and we shall be so happy. The truth is, Godfather, that I have been wrong. I have gone the wrong way to work. A little more love, and kindness, and forbearance, might have kept my sisters with us, might have led the little one to better tastes and pleasures, and have taught the other by experience the truth of the faith and hope and love which he now reviles. Oh, I have sinned! I have sinned! Let us turn back, Godfather Time, and begin again. And oh! drive very slowly, for partings come only too soon.'"

"'I am sorry,' said the old man in the same bitter tone as before, 'to disappoint your rather unreasonable wishes. What you say is admirably true, with this misfortune, that your good intentions are too late. Like the rest of the world you are ready to seize the opportunity when it is past. You should have been kind *then*. You should have advised *then*. You should have yielded *then*. You should have loved your brothers and sisters while you had them. It is too late now.'"

"With this he drove on, and spoke no more, and poor Melchior stared sadly out of the window. As he was gazing at the crowd, he suddenly saw the dog-cart, in which were his brother and his wretched companions. Oh, how old and worn he looked! and how ragged his clothes were! The men seemed to be trying to persuade him to do something that he did not like, and they began to quarrel; but in the midst of the dispute he turned his head and caught sight of the old coach; and Melchior seeing this, waved his hands, and beckoned with all his might. The brother seemed doubtful; but Melchior waved harder, and (was it fancy?) Time seemed to go slower. The brother made up his mind; he turned and jumped from the dog-cart as he had jumped from the old coach long ago, and ducking in and out among the horses and carriages, ran for his life. The men came after him; but he ran like the wind—pant, pant, nearer, nearer; at last the coach was reached, and Melchior seized the prodigal by his rags and dragged him in.

"'Oh, thank GOD, I have got you safe, my brother!'"

"But what a brother! with wasted body and sunken eyes; with the old curly hair turned to matted locks, that clung faster to his face than the rags did to his trembling limbs; what a sight for the opera-glasses of the crowd! What a subject for the tongues that were ever wagging, and complimenting, and backbiting, and lying, all in a breath, and without sense or scruple! What a sight and a subject for the fine friends, for whose good opinion Melchior had been so anxious? Do you think he was as anxious now? Do you think he was troubled by what they either saw or said; or was ashamed of the wretched prodigal lying among the cushions? I think not. I think that for the most foolish of us there are moments in life (of real joy or real sorrow) when we judge things by a higher standard, and care vastly little for what 'people say'. The only shame that Melchior felt was that his brother should have fared so hardly in the trials and temptations of the world outside, while he had sat at ease among the cushions of the old coach, that had been the home of both alike. Thank GOD, it was the home of both now! And poor Hop-o'-my-Thumb was on the front seat at last, with Melchior kneeling at his feet, and fondly stroking the head that rested against him.

"'Has powder come into fashion, brother?' he said. 'Your hair is streaked with white.'"

"'If it has,' said the other, laughing, 'your barber is better than mine, Melchior, for your head is as white as snow.'"

"'Is it possible? are we so old? has Time gone so very fast? But what are you staring at through the window? I shall be jealous of that crowd, brother.'"

"'I am not looking at the crowd,' said the prodigal in a low voice; 'but I see—'"

"'You see what?' said Melchior."

"'A figure in a cloak, gliding in and out—'"

"Melchior sprang up in horror. 'No! no!' he cried, hoarsely. 'No! surely no!'"

"Surely yes! Too surely the well-known figure came on; and the prodigal's sunken eyes looked more sunken still as he gazed. As for Melchior, he neither spoke nor moved, but stood in a silent agony, terrible to see. All at once a thought seemed to strike him; he seized his brother, and pushed him to the furthest corner of the seat, and then planted himself firmly at the door just as Death came up and put his hand into the coach. Then he spoke in a low steady voice, more piteous than cries or tears.

"'I humbly beseech you, good Death, if you must take one of us, to take me. I have had a long drive, and many comforts and blessings, and am willing if unworthy to go. He has suffered much, and had no pleasure; leave him for a little to enjoy the drive in peace, just for a very little; he has suffered so much, and I have been so much to blame; let me go instead of him.'"

"Alas for Melchior! It is decreed in the Providence of GOD, that, although the opportunities for doing good, which are in the power of every man, are beyond count or knowledge, yet, the opportunity once neglected, no man by any self-sacrifice can atone for those who have fallen or suffered by his negligence. Poor Melchior! An unalterable law made him the powerless spectator of the consequences of his neglected opportunities. 'No man may deliver his brother, or make agreement unto GOD for him, for it cost more to redeem their souls, so that he must let that alone for ever.' And is it ever so bitter to 'let alone,' as in a case where we might have acted and did not?

"Poor Melchior! In vain he laid both his hands in Death's outstretched palm; they fell to him again as if they had passed through air; he was pushed aside—Death passed into the coach—'one was taken and the other left.'"

"As the cloaked figure glided in and out among the crowd, many turned to look at his sad burden, though few heeded him. Much was said; but the general voice of the crowd was this: 'Ah! he is gone, is he? Well! a born rascal! It must be a great relief to his brother!' A conclusion which was about as wise, and about as near the truth, as the world's conclusions generally are. As for Melchior, he neither saw the figure nor heard the crowd, for he had fallen senseless among the cushions.

"When he came to his senses, he found himself lying still upon his face; and so bitter was his loneliness and grief, that he lay still and did not move. He was astonished, however, by the (as it seemed to him) unusual silence. The noise of the carriages had been deafening, and now there was not a sound. Was he deaf? or had the crowd gone? He opened his eyes. Was he blind? or had the night come? He sat right up, and shook himself, and looked again. The crowd *was* gone; so, for matter of that, was the coach; and so was Godfather Time. He had not been lying among cushions, but among pillows; he was not in any vehicle of any kind, but in bed. The room was dark, and very still; but through the 'barracks' window, which had no blind, he saw the winter sun pushing through the mist, like a red hot cannon-ball hanging in the frosty trees; and in the yard outside, the cocks were crowing.

"There was no longer any doubt that he was safe in his old home; but where were his brothers and sisters? With a beating heart he crept to the other end of the bed; and there lay the prodigal, but with no haggard cheeks or sunken eyes, no grey locks or miserable rags, but a rosy yellow-haired urchin fast asleep, with his head upon his arm. 'I took his pillow,' muttered Melchior, self-reproachfully.

"A few minutes later, young Hop-o'-my-Thumb (whom Melchior dared not lose sight of for fear he should melt away) seated comfortably on his brother's back, and wrapped up in a blanket, was making a tour of the 'barracks.'"

"'It's an awful lark,' said he, shivering with a mixture of cold and delight."

"If not exactly a *lark*, it was a very happy tour to Melchior, as, hope gradually changing into certainty, he recognized his brothers in one shapeless lump after the other in the little beds. There they all were, sleeping peacefully in a happy home, from the embryo hero to the embryo philosopher, who lay with the invariable book upon his pillow, and his hair looking (as it always did) as if he lived in a high wind.

"'I say,' whispered Melchior, pointing to him, 'what did he say the other day about being a parson?'"

"'He said he should like to be one,' returned Hop-o'-my-Thumb; 'but you said he would frighten away the congregation with his looks. And then, you know, he got very angry, and said he didn't know priests need be dandies, and that everybody was humbuggy alike, and thought of nothing but looks; but that he would be a philosopher like Diogenes, who cared for nobody, and was as ugly as an ape, and lived in a tub.'"

"'He will make a capital parson,' said Melchior, hastily, 'and I shall tell him so to-morrow. And when I'm squire here, he shall be vicar, and I'll subscribe to all his dodges without a grumble. I'm the eldest son. And, I say, don't you think we could brush his hair for him in a morning, till he learns to do it himself?'"

"'Oh, I will!' was the lively answer; 'I'm an awful dab at brushing. Look how I brush your best hat!'"

"'True,' said Melchior. 'Where are the girls to-night?'"

"'In the little room at the end of the long passage,' said Hop-o'-my-Thumb, trembling with increased chilliness and enjoyment. 'But you're never going there! we shall wake the company, and they will all come out to see what's the matter.'"

"'I shouldn't care if they did,' said Melchior, 'it would make it feel more real.'"

"As he did not understand this sentiment, Hop-o'-my-Thumb said nothing, but held on very tightly; and they crept softly down the cold grey passage in the dawn. The girls' door was open; for the girls were afraid of robbers, and left their bed-room door wide open at night, as a natural and obvious means of self-defence. The girls slept together; and the frill of the pale sister's prim little night-cap was buried in the other one's uncovered curls.

"'How you do tremble!' whispered Hop-o'-my-Thumb; 'are you cold?' This inquiry received no answer; and after some minutes he spoke again. 'I say, how very pretty they look! don't they?'

"But for some reason or other, Melchior seemed to have lost his voice; but he stooped down and kissed both the girls very gently, and then the two brothers crept back along the passage to the 'barracks.'"

"'One thing more,' said Melchior; and they went up to the mantelpiece. 'I will lend you my bow and arrows to-morrow, on one condition—'"

"'Anything!' was the reply, in an enthusiastic whisper."

"'That you take that old picture for a target, and never let me see it again.'"

"It was very ungrateful! but perfection is not in man; and there was something in Melchior's muttered excuse—

"'I couldn't stand another night of it.'"

"Hop-o'-my-Thumb was speedily put to bed again, to get warm, this time with both the pillows; but Melchior was too restless to sleep, so he resolved to have a shower-bath, and to dress. After which, he knelt down by the window, and covered his face with his hands.

"'He's saying very long prayers,' thought Hop-o'-my-Thumb, glancing at him from his warm nest; 'and what a jolly humour he is in this morning!'

"Still the young head was bent, and the handsome face hidden; and Melchior was finding his life every moment more real and more happy. For there was hardly a thing, from the well-filled 'barracks' to the brother bedfellow, that had been a hardship last night, which this morning did not seem a blessing. He rose at last, and stood in the sunshine, which was now pouring in; a smile was on his lips, and on his face were two drops, which, if they were water, had not come from the shower-bath, or from any bath at all."

*   *   *   *   *

"Is that the end?" inquired the young lady on his knee, as the story teller paused here."

"Yes, that is the end."

"It's a beautiful story," she murmured, thoughtfully; "but what an extraordinary one! I don't think I could have dreamt such a wonderful dream."

"Do you think you could have eaten such a wonderful supper?" said the friend, twisting his moustachios."

After this point, the evening's amusements were thoroughly successful. Richard took his smoking boots from the fire-place, and was called upon for various entertainments for which he was famous: such as the accurate imitation of a train just starting, in which two pieces of bone were used with considerable effect; as also of a bumble-bee, who (very much out of season) went buzzing about, and was always being caught with a heavy bang on the heads and shoulders of those who least expected it; all which specimens of his talents were received with due applause by his admiring brothers and sisters.

The bumble-bee had just been caught (for the twenty-first time) with a loud smack on brother Benjamin's ear, when the door opened, and Paterfamilias entered with Materfamilias (whose headache was better), and followed by the candles. A fresh log was then thrown upon the fire, the yule cakes and furmety were put upon the table, and everybody drew round to supper; and Paterfamilias announced that although he could not give the materials to play with, he had no objection now to a bowl of moderate punch for all, and that Richard might compound it. This was delightful; and as he sat by his father, ladling away to the rest, Adolphus Brown could hardly have felt more jovial, even with the champagne and ices.

The rest sat with radiant faces and shining heads in goodly order; and at the bottom of the table, by Materfamilias, was the friend, as happy in his unselfish sympathy as if his twenty-five sticks had come to life, and were supping with him. As happy—nearly—as if a certain woman's grave had never been dug under the southern sun that could not save her, and as if the children gathered round him were those of whose faces he had often dreamt, but might never see.

His health had been drunk, and everybody else's too, when, just as supper was coming to a close, Richard (who had been sitting in thoughtful silence for some minutes) got up with sudden resolution, and said,

"I want to propose Mr. What's-his-name's health on my own account. I want to thank him for his story, which had only one mistake in it. Melchior should have kept the effervescing papers to put into the beer; it's a splendid drink! Otherwise it was first-rate; though it hit me rather hard. I want to say that though I didn't mean all I said about being an only son (when a fellow gets put out he doesn't know what he means), yet I know I was quite wrong, and the story is quite right. I want particularly to say that I'm very glad there are so many of us, for the more, you know, the merrier. I wouldn't change father or mother, brothers or sisters, with any one in the world. It couldn't be better, we couldn't be happier. We are all together, and to-morrow is Christmas Day. Thank GOD."

It was very well said. It was a very good speech. It was very well and very good that while the blessings were with him, he could feel it to be so, and be grateful.

It was very well, and good also, that the friend, who had neither home nor kindred to be grateful for, had something else for which he could thank GOD as heartily. The thought of that something came to him then as he sat at his friend's table, filling his eyes with tears. It came to him next day as he knelt before GOD's altar, remembering in blessed fellowship that deed of love which is the foundation of all our hope and joy. It came to him when he went back to his lonely wandering life, and thought with tender interest of that boyish speech. It came—a whisper of consolation to silence envy and regret for ever.

"There *is* something far better. There *is* something far happier. There is a better Home than any earthly one, and a Family that shall never be divided."

THE BLACKBIRD'S NEST

"Let me not think an action mine own way,
But as Thy love shall sway,
Resigning up the rudder to Thy skill."

—GEORGE HERBERT

One day, when I was a very little girl (which is a long time ago), I made a discovery. The place where I made it was not very remote, being a holly-bush at the bottom of our garden; and the discovery was not a great one in itself, though I thought it very grand. I had found a blackbird's nest, with three young ones in it.

The discovery was made on this wise. I was sitting one morning on a log of wood opposite this holly-bush, reading the story of Goody Twoshoes, and thinking to myself how much I should like to be like her, and to go about in the village with a raven, a pigeon, and a lark on my shoulders, admired and talked about by everybody. All sorts of nonsense passed through my head as I sat, with the book on my lap, staring straight before me; and I was just fancying the kind condescension with which I would behave to everybody when I became a Goody Twoshoes, when I saw a bird come out of the holly-bush and fly away. It was a blackbird: there was no doubt of it; and it must have a nest in the tree, or why had it been there so long? Down went my book, and I flew to make my discovery. A blackbird's nest, with three young ones! I stood still at first in pure pleasure at the sight; and then, little by little, grand ideas came into my head.

I would be very kind to these little blackbirds, I thought; I would take them home out of this cold tree, and make a large nest of cotton wool (which would be much softer and better for them than to be where they were), and feed them, and keep them; and then, when they were full-grown, they would, of course, love me better than any one, and be very tame and grateful; and I should walk about with them on my shoulders, like Goody Twoshoes, and be admired by everybody; for, I am ashamed to say, most of my day dreams ended with this, *to be admired by everybody*. I was so wrapped up in these thoughts that I did not know, till his hands were laid upon my shoulders, that my friend, the curate of the village, had come up behind me. He lived next door to us, and often climbed over the wall that divided our garden to bring me flowers for my little bed. He was a tall, dark, not very young man; and the best hand at making fire-balloons, mending toys, and making a broken wax doll as good as new with a hot knitting needle, that you can imagine. I had heard grown-up people call him grave and silent, but he always laughed and talked to me.

"What are you doing, little woman?" he said.

"I have got a nest of poor little birds," I answered; "I am so sorry for them here in the cold; but they will be all right when I have got them indoors. I shall make them a beautiful nest of cotton wool, and feed them. Won't it be nice?"

I spoke confidently; for I had really so worked up my fancy that I felt quite a contemptuous pity for all the wretched little

Juliana Horatia Ewing

birds who were hatched every year without me to rear them. At the same time, I had a general idea that grown-up people always *did* throw cold water on splendid plans like mine; so I was more indignant than surprised when my friend the curate tried to show me that it was quite impossible to do as I wished. The end of all his arguments was that I must leave the nest in its place. But I had a great turn for disputing, and was not at all inclined to give up my point. "You told me on Sunday," I said, pertly, "that we were never too little to do kind things; let me do this."

"If I could be sure," he said, looking at me, "that you only wish to do a kind thing."

I got more angry and rude.

"Perhaps you think I want to kill them," I said.

He did not answer, but taking both my hands in his, said, gravely, "Tell me, my child, which do you wish most—to be kind to these poor little birds? or to have the honour and glory of having them, and bringing them up?"

"To be kind to them," said I, getting very red. "I don't want any honour and glory," and I felt ready to cry.

"Well, well," he said, smiling; "then I know you will believe me when I tell you that the kindest thing you can do for these little birds is to leave them where they are. And if you like, you can come and sit here every day till they are able to fly, and keep watch over the nest, that no naughty boy may come near it—the curate, for instance!" and he pulled a funny face. "That will be very kind."

"But they will never know, and I want them to like me," said I.

"I thought you only wanted to be kind," he answered. And then he began to talk very gently about different sorts of kindness, and that if I wished to be kind like a Christian, I must be kind without hoping for any reward, whether gratitude or anything else. He told me that the best followers of Jesus in all times had tried hard to do everything, however small, simply for GOD's sake, and to put themselves away. That they often began even their letters, etc., with such words, as, "Glory to GOD," to remind themselves that everything they did, to be perfect, must be done to GOD, and GOD alone. And that in doing good kind things even, they were afraid lest, though the thing was right, the wish to do it might have come from conceit or presumption.

"This self-devotion," he added, "is the very highest Christian life, and seems, I dare say, very hard for you even to understand, and much more so to put in practice. But we must all try for it in the best way we can, little woman; and for those who by GOD's grace really practised it, it was almost as impossible to be downcast or disappointed as if they were already in Heaven. They wished for nothing to happen to themselves but GOD's will; they did nothing but for GOD's glory. And so a very good bishop says, 'I have my end, whether I succeed or am disappointed.' So you will have your end, my child, in being kind to these little birds in the right way, and denying yourself, whether they know you or not."

I could not have understood all he said; but I am afraid I did not try to understand what I might have done; however, I said no more, and stood silent, while he comforted me with the promise of a new flower for my garden, called "hen and chickens," which he said I was to take care of instead of the little blackbirds.

When he was gone I went back to the holly-bush, and stood gazing at the nest, and nursing angry thoughts in my heart.

Juliana Horatia Ewing

"What a *preach*," I thought, "about nothing! as if there could be any conceit and presumption in taking care of three poor little birds! The curate must forget that I was growing into a big girl; and as to not knowing how to feed them, I knew as well as he did that birds lived upon worms, and liked bread-crumbs." And so *thinking wrong* ended (as it almost always does) in *doing wrong*: and I took the three little blackbirds out of the nest, popped them into my pocket-handkerchief, and ran home. And I took some trouble to keep them out of everyone's sight—even out of my mother's; for I did not want to hear any more "grown-up" opinions on the matter.

I filled a basket with cotton wool, and put the birds inside, and took them into a little room downstairs, where they would be warm. Before I went to bed I put two or three worms, and a large supply of soaked bread-crumbs, in the nest, close to their little beaks. "What can they want more?" thought I in my folly; but conscience is apt to be restless when one is young, and I could not feel quite comfortable in bed, though I got to sleep at last, trying to fancy myself Goody Twoshoes, with three sleek full-fledged blackbirds on my shoulders.

In the morning, as soon as I could slip away, I went to my pets. Any one may guess what I found; but I believe no one can understand the shock of agony and remorse that I felt. There lay the worms that I had dug up with reckless cruelty; there was the wasted bread; and there, above all, lay the three little blackbirds, cold and dead!

I do not know how long I stood looking at the victims of my presumptuous wilfulness; but at last I heard a footstep in the passage, and fearing to be caught, I tore out of the house, and down to my old seat near the holly-bush, where I flung myself on the ground, and "wept bitterly." At last I heard the well-known sound of some one climbing over the wall; and then the curate stood before me, with the plant of "hen and chickens" in his hands. I jumped up, and shrank away from him.

"Don't come near me," I cried; "the blackbirds are dead;" and I threw myself down again.

I knew from experience that few things roused the anger of my friend so strongly as to see or hear of animals being ill-treated. I had never forgotten, one day when I was out with him, his wrath over a boy who was cruelly beating a donkey; and now I felt, though I could not see, the expression of his face, as he looked at the holly-bush and at me, and exclaimed, "You took them!" And then added, in the low tone in which he always spoke when angry, "And the mother-bird has been wandering all night round this tree, seeking her little ones in vain, not to be comforted, because they are not! Child, child! has GOD the Father given life to His creatures for you to destroy it in this reckless manner?"

His words cut my heart like a knife; but I was too utterly wretched already to be much more miserable; I only lay still and moaned. At last he took pity, and lifting me up on to his knee, endeavoured to comfort me.

This was not, however, an easy matter. I knew much better than he did how very naughty I had been; and I felt that I had murdered the poor tender little birds.

"I can never, never, forgive myself!" I sobbed.

"But you must be reasonable," he said. "You gave way to your vanity and wilfulness, and persuaded yourself that you only wished to be kind to the blackbirds; and you have been punished. Is it not so?"

"O yes!" I cried; "I am so wicked! I wish I were as good as you are!"

"As I am!"—he began.

I was too young then to understand the sharp tone of self-reproach in which he spoke. In my eyes he was perfection; only perhaps a little *too* good. But he went on:—

"Do you know, this fault of yours reminds me of a time when I was just as wilful and conceited, just as much bent upon doing the great duty of helping others in my own grand fashion, rather than in the humble way which GOD's Providence pointed out, only it was in a much more serious matter; I was older, too, and so had less excuse. I am almost tempted to tell you about it; not that our cases are really quite alike, but that the punishment which met my sin was so unspeakably bitter in comparison with yours, that you may be thankful to have learnt a lesson of humility at smaller cost."

I did not understand him—in fact, I did not understand many things that he said, for he had a habit of talking to me as if he were speaking to himself; but I had a general idea of his meaning, and said (very truly), "I cannot fancy you doing wrong."

I was puzzled again by the curious expression of his face; but he only said, "Shall I tell you a story?"

I knew his stories of old, and gave an eager "Yes."

"It is a sad one," he said.

"I do not think I should like a very funny one just now," I replied. "Is it true?"

"Quite," he answered. "It is about myself." He was silent for a few moments, as if making up his mind to speak; and then, laying his head, as he sometimes did, on my shoulder, so that I could not see his face, he began.

"When I was a boy (older than you, so I ought to have been better), I might have been described in the words of Scripture—I was 'the only son of my mother, and she was a widow.' We were badly off, and she was very delicate, nay, ill—more ill, GOD knows, than I had any idea of. I had long been used to the sight of the doctor once or twice a week, and to her being sometimes better and sometimes worse; and when our old servant lectured me for making a noise, or the doctor begged that she might not be excited or worried, I fancied that doctors and nurses always did say things of that sort, and that there was no particular need to attend to them.

"Not that I was unfeeling to my dear mother, for I loved her devotedly in my wilful worldly way. It was for her sake that I had been so vexed by the poverty into which my father's death had plunged us. For her sake I worried her, by grumbling before her at our narrow lodgings and lost comforts. For her sake, child, in my madness, I wasted the hours in which I might have soothed, and comforted, and waited on her, in dreaming of wild schemes for making myself famous and rich, and giving her back all and more than she had lost. For her sake I fancied myself pouring money at her feet, and loading her with luxuries, while she was praying for me to our common Father, and laying up treasure for herself in Heaven.

"One day I remember, when she was remonstrating with me over a bad report which the schoolmaster had given of me (he said I could work, but wouldn't), my vanity overcame my prudence, and I told her that I thought some fellows were made to 'fag,' and some not; that I had been writing a poem in my dictionary the day that I had done so badly, and that I hoped to be a poet long before my master had composed a grammar. I can see now her sorrowful face as, with tears in her eyes, she told me that all 'fellows' alike were made to do their duty 'before GOD, and Angels, and Men.' That it was by improving the little events and opportunities of every day that men became great, and not by neglecting them for their own presumptuous fancies. And she entreated me to strive to do my duty, and to leave the rest with GOD. I listened, however, impatiently to what I called a 'jaw' or a 'scold,' and then (knowing the tender interest she took in all I did) I tried to coax her by offering to read my poem. But she answered with just severity, that what she wished was to see me a good man, not a great one; and that she would rather see my exercises duly written than fifty poems composed at the expense of my neglected duty. Then she warned me tenderly of the misery which my conceit would bring upon me, and bade me, when I said my evening prayers, to add that prayer of King David, 'Keep Thy servant from presumptuous sins, lest they get the dominion over me.'"

"Alas! they had got the dominion over me already, too strongly for her words to take any hold. 'She won't even look at my poem,' I thought, and hurried proudly from the room, banging one door and leaving another open. And I silenced my uneasy conscience by fresh dreams of making my fortune and hers. But the punishment came at last. One day the doctor took me into a room alone, and told me as gently as he could what everyone but myself knew already—my mother was dying. I cannot tell you, child, how the blow fell upon me—how, at first, I utterly disbelieved its truth! It seemed *impossible* that the only hope of my life, the object of all my schemes and fancies, was to be taken away. But I was awakened at last, and resolved that, GOD helping me, while she did live, I would be a better son. I can now look back with thankfulness on the few days we were together. I never left her. She took her food and medicine from my hand; and I received my First Communion with her on the day she died. The day before, kneeling by her bed, I had confessed all the sin and vanity of my heart and those miserable dreams; had destroyed with my own hand all my papers, and had resolved that I would apply to my studies, and endeavour to obtain a scholarship and the necessary preparation for Holy Orders. It was a just ambition, little woman, undertaken humbly, in the fear of GOD, and in the path of duty; and I accomplished it years after, when I had nothing left of my mother but her memory."

The curate was silent, and I felt, rather than saw, that the tears which were wetting my frock had not come from my own eyes, though I was crying bitterly. I flung my arms round his neck, and hugged him tight.

"Oh, I am so sorry!" I sobbed; "so very, very sorry!"

We became quieter after a bit; and he lifted up his head and smiled, and called himself a fool for making me sad, and told me not to tell any one what he had told me, and what babies we had been, except my mother.

"Tell her *everything* always," he said.

I soon cheered up, particularly as he took me over the wall, and into his workshop, and made a coffin for the poor little blackbirds, which we lined with cotton-wool and scented with musk, as a mark of respect. Then he dug a deep hole in the garden and we buried them, and made a fine high mound of earth, and put the "hen and chicken" plants all round. And that night, sitting on my mother's knee, I told her "everything," and shed a few more tears of sorrow and repentance in her arms.

*   *   *   *   *

Many years have passed since then, and many showers of rain have helped to lay the mound flat with the earth, so that the "hen and chickens" have run all over it, and made a fine plot. The curate and his mother have met at last; and I have transplanted many flowers that he gave me to his grave. I sometimes wonder if, in his perfect happiness, he knows, or cares to know, how often the remembrance of his story has stopped the current of conceited day-dreams, and brought me back to practical duty with the humble prayer, "Keep Thy servant also from presumptuous sins."

FRIEDRICH'S BALLAD

A TALE OF THE FEAST OF ST. NICHOLAS

"Ne pinger ne scolpir fia piu che queti,
L'anima volta a quell' Amor divino
Ch'asserse a prender noi in Croce le braccia."

"Painting and Sculpture's aid in vain I crave,
My one sole refuge is that Love divine
Which from the Cross stretched forth its arms to save."

—Written by MICHAEL ANGELO *at the age of 83*

"So be it," said one of the council, as he rose and addressed the others. "It is now finally decided. The Story Woman is to be walled up."

The council was not an ecclesiastical one, and the woman condemned to the barbarous and bygone punishment of being "walled up" was not an offending nun. In fact the Story Woman (or *Maerchen-Frau* as she is called in Germany) may be taken to represent the imaginary personage who is known in England by the name of Mother Bunch, or Mother Goose; and it was in this instance the name given by a certain family of children to an old book of ballads and poems, which they were accustomed to read in turn with special solemnities, on one particular night in the year; the reader for the time being having a peculiar costume, and the title of "Maerchen-Frau," or Mother Bunch, a name which had in time been familiarly adopted for the ballad-book itself.

This book was not bound in a fashionable colour, nor illustrated by a fashionable artist; the Chiswick Press had not set up a type for it, and Hayday's morocco was a thing unknown. It had not, in short, one of those attractions with which in these days books are surrounded, whose insides do not always fulfil the promise of the binding. If, however, it was on these points inferior to modern volumes, it had on others the advantage. It did not share a precarious favour with a dozen rivals in mauve, to be supplanted ere the year was out by twelve new ones in magenta. It was never thrown aside with the contemptuous remark,—"I've read that!" On the contrary, it always had been to its possessors, what (from the best Book downwards) a good book always should be, a friend, and not an acquaintance—not to be too readily criticized, but to be loved and trusted. The pages were yellow and worn, not with profane ill-usage, but with honourable wear and tear; and the mottled binding presented much such an appearance as might be expected from a book that had been pressed under the pillow of one reader, and in the pocket of another; that had been wept over and laughed over, and warmed by winter fires, and damped in the summer grass, and had in general seen as much of life as the venerable book in question. It was not the property of one member of the family, but the joint possession of all. It was not *mine*, but *ours*, as the inscription, "For the Children," written on the blank leaf testified; which inscription was hereafter to be a pathetic memorial to aged eyes of days when "the children" were not yet separated, and took their pleasures, like their meals, together.

And after all this, with the full consent of a council of the owners, the *Maerchen-Frau* was to be "walled up."

But before I attempt to explain, or in any way excuse this seemingly ungracious act, it may be well to give some account of the doers thereof. Well, then:—

Providence had blessed a certain respectable tradesman, in a certain town in Germany, with a large and promising family of children. He had married very early the beloved of his boyhood, and had been left a widower with one motherless baby almost before he was a man. A neighbour, with womanly compassion, took pity upon this desolate father, and more desolate child; and it was not until she had nursed the babe in her own house through a dangerous sickness, and had for long been chief adviser to the parent, that he awoke to the fact that she had become necessary to him, and they were married.

Of this union came a family of eight, the two eldest of whom were laid in turn in the quiet grave. The others survived, and, with the first wife's daughter, made a goodly family party, which sometimes sorely taxed the resources of the tradesman to provide for, though his business was good and his wife careful. They scrambled up, however, as children are wont to do in such circumstances; and at the time our story opens the youngest had turned his back upon babyhood, and Marie, the eldest, had reached that pinnacle of childish ambition—she was "grown up."

A very good Marie she was, and always had been; from the days when she ran to school with a little knapsack on her back, and her fair hair hanging down in two long plaits, to the present time, when she tenderly fastened that same knapsack on to the shoulders of a younger sister; and when the plaits had for long been reclaimed from their vagrant freedom, and coiled close to her head.

"Our Marie is not clever," said one of the children, who flattered himself that *he was* a bit of a genius; "our Marie is not clever, but also she is never wrong."

It is with this same genius that our story has chiefly to do.

Friedrich was a child of unusual talent; a fact which, happily for himself, was not discovered till he was more than twelve years old. He learnt to read very quickly; and when he was once able, read every book on which he could lay his hands, and in his father's house the number was not great. When Marie was a child, the school was kept by a certain old man, very gentle and learned in his quiet way. He had been fond of his fair-haired pupil, and when she was no longer a scholar, had passed many an odd hour in imparting to her a slight knowledge of Latin, and of the great Linnaeus' system of botany. He was now dead, and his place filled by a less sympathizing pedagogue; and Friedrich listened with envious ears to his more fortunate sister's stories of her friend and master.

"So he taught you Latin—that great language! And botany—which is a science!" the child would exclaim with envious admiration, when he had heard for the thousandth time every particular of the old schoolmaster's kindness.

And Marie would answer calmly, as she "refooted" one of the father's stockings, "We did a good deal of the grammar, which I fear I have forgotten, and I learnt by heart a few of the Psalms in Latin, which I remember well. Also we commenced the system of Mr. Linnaeus, but I was very stupid, and ever preferred those plates which pictured the flower itself to those which gave the torn pieces, and which he thought most valuable. But, above all, he taught me to be good; and though I have forgotten many of his lessons, there are words and advice of his which I heeded little then, but which come back and teach me now. Father once heard the Burgomaster say he was a genius, but I know that he was good, and that is best of all;" with which, having turned the heel of her stocking, Marie would put it out of reach of the kitten, and lay the table for dinner.

And Friedrich—poor Friedrich!—groaning inwardly at his sister's indifference to her great opportunities for learning, would speculate to himself on the probable fate of each volume in the old schoolmaster's library, which had been sold when he, Friedrich, was but three years old. Thus, in these circumstances, the boy expressed his feelings with moderation when he said, "Our Marie is not clever, but also she is never wrong."

If the schoolmaster was dead, however, Friedrich was not, nevertheless, friendless. There was a certain bookseller in his native town, for whom in his spare time he ran messages, and who in return was glad to let him spend his playhours and half-holidays among the books in his shop. There, perched at the top of the shelves on a ladder, or crouched upon his toes at the bottom, he devoured some volumes and dipped into others; but what he liked best was poetry, and this not uncommon taste with many young readers was with this one a mania. Wherever the sight of verses met his eye, there he fastened and read greedily.

One day, a short time before my story opens, he found, in his wanderings from shelf to shelf, some nicely-bound volumes, one of which he opened, and straightway verses of the most attractive-looking metre met his eye, not, however, in German, but in a fair round Roman text, and, alas! in a language which he did not understand. There were customers in the shop, so he stood still in the corner with his nose almost resting on the bookshelf, staring fiercely at the page, as if he would force the meaning out of those fair clear-looking verses. When the last beard had vanished through the doorway, Friedrich came up to the counter, book in hand.

"Well, now?" said the comfortable bookseller, with a round German smile.

"This book," said the boy; "in what language is it?"

The man stuck his spectacles on his nose, and smiled again.

"It is Italian, and these are the sonnets of Petrarch, my child. The edition is a fine one, so be careful." Friedrich went back to his place, sighing heavily. After a while he came out again.

"Well now, what is it?" said the bookseller, cheerfully.

"Have you an Italian grammar?"

"Only this," said the other, as he picked a book from the shelf and laid it on the counter with a twinkle in his eye. The boy opened it and looked up disappointed.

"It is all Italian," said he.

"No, no," was the answer; "it is in French and Italian, and was printed at Paris. But what wouldst thou with a grammar, my child?"

The boy blushed as if he had been caught stealing, and said hastily—

"I *must* read those poems, and I cannot if I do not learn the language."

"And thou wouldst read Petrarch with a grammar," shouted the bookseller; "ho! ho! ho!"

"And a dictionary," said Friedrich; "why not?"

"Why not?" repeated the other, with renewed laughter. "Why not? Because to learn a language, my Friedrich, one must have a master, and exercises, and a phrase-book, and progressive reading-lessons with vocabulary; and, in short, one must learn a language in the way everybody else learns it; that is why not, my Friedrich."

"Everybody is nobody," said Friedrich, hotly; "at least nobody worth caring for. If I had a grammar and a dictionary, I would read those beautiful poems."

"Hear him!" said the cheerful little bookseller. "He will read Petrarch. He! If my volumes stop in the shelves till thou canst read them, my child—ho! ho! ho!" and he rubbed his brushy little beard with glee.

Friedrich's temper was not by nature of the calmest, and this conversation rubbed its tenderest points. He answered almost fiercely—

"Take care of your volumes. If I live, and they *do* stop in the shelves, I will buy them of you some day. Remember!" and he turned sharply round to hide the tears which had begun to fall.

For a moment the good shopkeeper's little mouth became as round as his round little eyes and his round little face; then he laid his hands on the counter, and jumping neatly over flung his dead weight on to Friedrich, and embraced him heartily.

"My poor child! (a kiss)—would that it had pleased Heaven to make thee the son of a nobleman—(another kiss). But hear me. A man in Berlin is now compiling an Italian grammar. It is to be out in a month or two. I shall have a copy, and thou shalt see it; and if ever thou canst read Petrarch I will give thee my volumes—(a volley of kisses). And now, as thou hast stayed so long, come into the little room and dine with me." With which invitation the kind-hearted German released his young friend and led him into the back room, where they buried the memory of Petrarch in a mess of vegetables and melted butter.

It may be added here, that the Petrarchs remained on the shelf, and that years afterwards the round-faced little bookseller redeemed his promise with pride.

Of these visits the father was to all intents and purposes ignorant. He knew that Friedrich went to see the bookseller, and that the bookseller was good-natured to him; but he never dreamt that his son read the books with which his neighbour's shop was lined, and he knew nothing of the wild visions which that same shop bred and nourished in the mind of his boy, and which made the life outside its doorstep seem a dream. The father and son saw that life from different points of view. The boy felt that he was more talented than other boys, and designed himself for a poet; the tradesman saw that the boy was more talented than other boys, and designed him for the business; and the opposite nature of these determinations was the one great misery of Friedrich's life.

If, however, this source of the child's sorrows was a secret one, and not spoken of to his brothers and sisters, or even to his friend the bookseller, equally secret also were the sources of his happiness. No eye but his own ever beheld those scraps of paper which he begged from the bookseller, and covered with childish efforts at verse-making. No one shared the happiness of those hours, of which perhaps a quarter was spent in working at the poem, and three-fourths were given to the day-dreams of the poet; or knew that the wild fancies of his brain made Friedrich's nights more happy than his days. By day he was a child (his family, with some reason, said a tiresome one), by night he was a man, and a great man. He visited the courts of Europe, and received compliments from Royalty; *his* plays were acted in the theatres; *his* poems stood on the shelves of the booksellers; he made his family rich (the boy was too young to wish for money for himself); he made everybody happy, and himself famous.

Fame! that was the word that rang in his ears and danced before his eyes as the hours of the night wore on, and he lived through a glorious lifetime. And so, when the mother, candle in hand, came round like a guardian angel among the sleeping children, to see that "all was right," he—poor child!—must feign to be sleeping on his face, to hide the traces of the tears which he had wept as he composed the epitaph which was to grace the monument of the famous Friedrich—, poet, philosopher, etc. Whoever doubts the possibility of such exaggerated folly, has never known an imaginative childhood, or wept over those unreal griefs, which are not the less bitter at the time from being remembered afterwards with a mixture of shame and amusement. Happy or unhappy, however, in his dreams the boy was great, and this was enough; for Friedrich was vain, as everyone is tempted to be who feels himself in any way singular and unlike those about him. He revelled in the honours which he showered upon himself, and so—the night was happy; and so—the day was unwelcome when he was smartly bid to get up and put on his stockings, and found Fame gone and himself a child again, without honour, in his own country, and in his father's house.

These sad dreams (sad in their uselessness) were destined,

however, to do him some good at last; and, oddly enough, the childish council that condemned the ballad-book decided his fate also. This was how it happened.

The children were accustomed, as we have said, to celebrate the Feast of St. Nicholas by readings from their beloved book. St. Nicholas's Day (the 6th of December) has for years been a favourite festival with the children in many parts of the Continent. In France, the children are diligently taught that St. Nicholas comes in the night down the chimney, and fills the little shoes (which are ranged there for the purpose) with sweetmeats or rods, according to his opinion of their owner's conduct during the past year. The Saint is supposed to travel through the air, and to be followed by an ass laden with two panniers, one of which contains the good things, and the other the birch, and he leaves his ass at the top of the chimney and comes down alone. The same belief is entertained in Holland; and in some parts of Germany he is even believed to carry off bad boys and girls in his sack, answering in this respect to our English Bogy.

The day, as may be supposed, is looked forward to with no small amount of anxiety; very clean and tidy are the little shoes placed by the young expectants; and their parents— who have threatened and promised in St. Nicholas's name for a year past—take care that, with one sort of present or the other, the shoes are well filled. The great question—rods or sweetmeats—is, however, finally settled for each individual before breakfast-time on the great day; and before dinner, despite maternal warnings, most of the said sweetmeats have been consumed. And so it came to pass that Friedrich and his brothers and sisters had hit upon a plan for ending the day, with the same spirit and enjoyment with which it opened.

The mother, by a little kind manoeuvring, generally induced the father to sup and take his evening pipe with a neighbour, for the tradesman was one of those whose presence is rather a "wet blanket" upon all innocent folly and fun. Then she good-naturedly took herself off to household matters, and the children were left in undisturbed possession of the stove, round which they gathered with the book, and the game commenced. Each in turn read whichever poem he preferred; and the reader for the time being, was wrapt in a huge hood and cloak, kept for the purpose, and was called the "Maerchen-Frau," or Story Woman. Sometimes the song had a chorus, which all the children sang to whichever suited best of the thousand airs that are always floating in German brains. Sometimes, if the ballad was a favourite one, the others would take part in any verses that contained a dialogue. This was generally the case with some verses in the pet ballad of Bluebeard, at that exciting point where Sister Anne is looking from the castle window. First the Maerchen-Frau read in a sonorous voice—

"Schwester Aennchen, siehst du nichts?"
(Sister Anne, do you see nothing?)

Then the others replied for Anne—

"Staeubchen fliegen, Graeschen wehen."
(A little dust flies, a little grass waves.)

Again the Maerchen-Frau—

"Aennchen, laesst sich sonst nichts sehen?"
(Little Anne, is there nothing else to be seen?)

And the unsatisfactory reply—

"Schwesterchen, sonst seh' ich nichts!"
(Little sister, I see nothing else!)

After this the Maerchen-Frau finished the ballad alone, and the conclusion was received with shouts of applause and laughter, that would have considerably astonished the good father, could he have heard them, and that did sometimes oblige the mother to call order from the loft above, just for propriety's sake; for, in truth, the good woman loved to hear them, and often hummed in with a chorus to herself as she turned over the clothes among which she was busy.

At last, however, after having been for years the crowning enjoyment of St. Nicholas's Day, the credit of the Maerchen-Frau was doomed to fade. The last reading had been rather a failure, not because the old ballad-book was supplanted by a new one, or because the children had outgrown its histories; perhaps—though they did not acknowledge it—Friedrich was in some degree to blame.

His increasing knowledge, the long readings in the bookseller's shop, which his brothers and sisters neither shared nor knew of, had given him a feeling of contempt for the one book on which they feasted from year to year; and his part, as Maerchen-Frau, had been on this occasion more remarkable for yawns than for anything else. The effect of this failure was not confined to that day. Whenever the book was brought out, there was the same feeling that the magic of it was gone, and very greatly were the poor children disquieted by the fact.

At last, one summer's day, in the year of which we are writing, one of the boys was struck, as he fancied, by a brilliant idea; and as brilliant ideas on any subject are precious, he lost no time in summoning a council of his brothers and sisters in the garden. It was a half-holiday, and they soon came trooping round the great linden tree—where the bees were already in full possession—and the youngest girl, who was but six years old, bore the book hugged fast in her two arms.

The boy opened the case—as lawyers say—by describing the loss of interest in their book since the last Feast of St. Nicholas. "This did not," he said, "arise from any want of love to the stories themselves, but from the fact of their knowing them so well. Whatever ballad the Maerchen-Frau chose, every line of it was so familiar to each one of them that it seemed folly to repeat it. In these circumstances it was evident that the greatest compliment they could pay the stories was to forget them, and he had a plan for attaining this desirable end. Let them deny themselves now for their future pleasure; let them put away the Maerchen-Frau till next St. Nicholas's Day, and, in the meantime, let each of them do his best to forget as much of it as he possibly could." The speaker ceased, and in the silence the bees above droned as if in answer, and then the children below shouted applause until the garden rang.

But now came the question, where was the Maerchen-Frau to be put? and for this the suggestive brother had also an idea. He had found certain bricks in the thick old garden wall which were loose, and when taken out there was a hole which was quite the thing for their purpose. Let them wrap the book carefully up, put it in the hole, and replace the bricks. This was his proposal, and he sat down. The bees droned above, the children shouted below, and the proposal was carried amid general satisfaction. "So be it," said the suggestor, in conclusion. "It is now finally decided. The Maerchen-Frau is to be walled up."

And walled up she was forthwith, but not without a parting embrace from each of her judges, and possibly some slight latent faith in the suggestion of one of the party that perhaps St. Nicholas would put a new inside and new stories into her before next December.

"I don't think I should like a new inside, though," doubted the child before mentioned, with a shake of her tiny plaits, "or new stories either."

As this quaint little Fraeulein went into the house she met Friedrich, who came from the bookseller's.

"Friedrich," said she, in a solemn voice, "we have walled up the 'Maerchen-Frau.'"

"Have you, *Schwesterchen*?"

This was Friedrich's answer; but it may safely be stated that, if any one had asked him what it was his sister had told him, he would have been utterly unable to reply.

He had been to the bookseller's!

The summer passed, and the children kept faithfully to their resolve. The little sister sometimes sat by the wall and comforted the Maerchen-Frau inside, with promises of coming out soon; but not a brick was touched. There was something pathetic in the children's voluntary renouncement of their one toy. The father was too absent and the mother too busy, to notice its loss; Marie missed it and made inquiries of the children, but she was implored to be silent, and discreetly held her tongue. Winter drew on, and for some time a change was visible in the manners of one of the children; he seemed restless and uncomfortable, as if something preyed upon his mind. At last he was induced to unburden himself to the others, when it was discovered that he couldn't forget the poems in "Maerchen-Frau." This was the grievance.

"It seems as if I did it on purpose," groaned he in self-indignation. "The nearer the time comes, and the more I try to forget, the clearer I remember them everyone. You know my pet is Bluebeard; well, I thought I would forget that altogether, every word: and then when my turn came to be Maerchen-Frau I would take it for my piece. And now, of all the rest, this is just the one that runs in my head. It is quite as if I did it on purpose."

Involuntarily the company—who appeared to have forgotten it as little as he—struck up in a merry tune—

"Blaubart war ein reicher Mann," etc.[A]

"Oh, don't!" groaned the victim. "That's just how it goes in my head all along, especially the verse—

"Stark war seines Koerpers Ban,
Feurig waren seine Blicke,
Aber ach!—ein Missgeschicke!—
Aber ach! sein Bart war blau."[B]

"On Sunday, when the preacher gave out the text, I was looking at him, and it came so strongly into my head that I nearly said it out loud—'But ah! his beard was blue!' To-day the schoolmaster asked me a question about Solomon. I could remember nothing but 'Ah! his beard was blue!' I have tried this week with all my might; and the harder I try, the better I remember every word. It is dreadful."

[Footnote A: "Bluebeard was a rich man."]

[Footnote B:

"Strong was the build of his body,
Fiery were his glances,
But ah!—disaster!—
But ah! his beard was blue."]

It was dreadful; but he was somewhat comforted to learn that the memories of his brothers and sisters were as perverse as his own. Those ballads were not to be easily forgotten. They refused to give up their hold on the minds they had nourished and amused so long.

One and all the children were really distressed, with the exception of Friedrich, who had, as usual, given about half his attention to the subject in hand; and who now sat absently humming to himself the account of Bluebeard's position and character, as set forth in Gotter's ballad.

The others came to the conclusion that there was but one hope left—that St. Nicholas might have put some new ballads into the old book—and one and all they made for the hiding-place, followed at a feebler pace by the little Fraeulein, who ran with her lips tightly shut, her hands clenched, and her eyes wide open with a mixture of fear and expectation. The bricks were removed, the book unwrapped, but alas! everything was the same, even to the rough woodcut of Bluebeard himself, in the act of sharpening his scimitar. There was no change, except that the volume was rather the worse for damp. It was thrown down with a murmur of disappointment, but seized immediately by the little Fraeulein, who flung herself upon it in a passion of tears and embraces. Hers was the only faithful affection; the charm of the Maerchen-Frau was gone.

They were all out of humour with this, and naturally looked about for some one to find fault with. Friedrich was at hand, and so they fell upon him and reproached him for his want of sympathy with their vexation. The boy awoke from a brown study, and began to defend himself:—"He was very sorry," he said; "but he couldn't see the use of making such a great fuss about a few old ballads, that after all were nothing so very wonderful."

This was flat heresy, and he was indignantly desired to say where any were to be got like them—where even *one* might be found, when St. Nicholas could not provide them? Friedrich was even less respectful to the idea of St. Nicholas, and said something which, translated into English, would look very like the word *humbug*. This was no answer to the question "where were they to get a ballad?" and a fresh storm came upon his head; whereupon being much goaded, and in a mixture of vanity and vexation of spirit, he let out the fact that "he thought he could write one almost as good himself."

This turned the current of affairs. The children had an instinctive belief in Friedrich's talents, to which their elders had not attained. The faith of childhood is great; and they saw no reason why he should not be able to do as he said, and so forthwith began to pet and coax him as unmercifully as they had scolded five minutes before.

"Beloved Friedrich; dear little brother! *Do* write one for us. We know thou canst!"

"I cannot," said Friedrich. "It is all nonsense. I was only joking."

"It is not nonsense; we know thou canst! Dear Fritz—just to please us!"

"Do!" said another. "It was only yesterday the mother was saying, 'Friedrich can do nothing useful!' But when thou hast written a poem thou wilt have done more than any one in the house—ay, or in the town. And when thou hast written one poem thou wilt write more, and be like Hans Sachs, and the Twelve Wise Masters thou hast told us of so often."

Friedrich had read many of the verses of the Cobbler Poet, but the name of Hans Sachs awakened no thought in his mind. He had heard nothing of that speech but one sentence, and it decided him.

Friedrich can do nothing useful. "I will see what I can do," he said, and walked hastily away. Down the garden, out into the road, away to the mill, where he could stand by the roaring water and talk aloud without being heard.

"Friedrich can do nothing useful. Yes, I will write a ballad."

He went home, got together some scraps of paper, and commenced.

In half-a-dozen days he began as many ballads, and tore them up one and all. He beat his brains for plots, and was satisfied with none. He had a fair maiden, a cruel father, a wicked sister, a handsome knight, and a castle on the Rhine; and so plunged into a love story with a moonlight meeting, an escape on horseback, pursuit, capture, despair, suicide, and a ghostly apparition that floated over the river, and wrung her hands under the castle window. It seems impossible for an author to do more for his heroine than take her out of the world, and bring her back again; but our poet was not content. He had not come himself to the sentiment of life, and felt a rough boyish disgust at the maundering griefs of his hero and heroine, who, moreover, were unpleasantly like every other hero and heroine that he had ever read of under similar circumstances; and if there was one thing more than another that Friedrich was determined to be, it was to be original.

He had no half hopes. With the dauntlessness of young ambition, he determined to do his very best, and that that best should be better than anything that ever had been done by any one.

Having failed with the sentimental, he tried to write something funny. Surely such child's tales as Bluebeard, Cinderella, etc., were easy enough to write. He would make a *Kindeslied*—a child's song. But he was mistaken; to write a new nursery ballad was the hardest task of all. Time after time he struggled; and, at last, one day when he had written and destroyed a longer effort than usual, he went to bed in hopeless despair.

His disappointment mingled with his dreams. He dreamt that he was in the bookseller's shop hunting among the shelves for some scraps of paper on which he had written. He could not find them, he thought, but came across the Petrarch volumes in their beautiful binding. He opened one and saw—not a word of that fair-looking Italian, but—his own ballad that he could not write, written and printed in good German character with his name on the title-page. He took it in his hands and went out of the shop, and as he did so it seemed to him, in his dream, that he had become a man. He dreamt that as he came down the steps, the people in the street gathered round him and cheered and shouted. The women held up their children to look at him; he was a Great Man! He thought that he turned back into the shop and went up to the counter. There sat the smiling little bookseller as natural as life, who smiled and bowed to him, as Friedrich had a hundred times seen him bow and smile to the bearded men who came in to purchase.

"How many have you sold of this?" said Friedrich, in his dream.

"Forty thousand!" with another smile and bow.

Forty thousand! It seemed to him that all the world must have read it. This was Fame.

He went out of the shop, through the shouting market-place, and home, where his father led him in and offered pipes and a mug of ale, as if he were the Burgomaster. He sat down, and when his mother came in, rose to embrace her, and, doing so, knocked down the mug. Crash! it went on the floor with a loud noise, which woke him up; and then he found himself in bed, and that he had thrown over the mug of water which he had put by his bedside to drink during the thirsty feverish hours that he lay awake.

He was not a great man, but a child.

He had not written a ballad, but broken a mug.

"Friedrich can do nothing useful."

He buried his face, and wept bitterly.

In time, his tears were dried, and as it was very early he lay awake and beat his brains. He had added nothing to his former character but the breaking of a piece of crockery. Something must be done. No more funny ballads now. He would write something terrible—miserable; something that should make other people weep as he had wept. He was in a very tragic humour indeed. He would have a hero who should go into the world to seek his fortune, and come back to find his lady-love in a nunnery; but that was an old story. Well, he would turn it the other way, and put the hero into a monastery; but that wasn't new. Then he would shut both of them up, and not let them meet again till one was a monk and the other a nun, which would be grievous enough in all reason; but this was the oldest of all. Friedrich gave up love stories on the spot. It was clearly not his *forte*.

Then he thought he would have a large family of brothers and sisters, and kill them all by a plague. But, besides the want of further incident, this idea did not seem to him sufficiently sad. Either from its unreality, or from their better faith, the idea of death does not possess the same gloom for the young that it does for those older minds that have a juster sense of the value of human life, and are, perhaps, more heavily bound in the chains of human interests.

No; the plague story might be pathetic, but it was not miserable—not miserable enough at any rate for Friedrich.

In truth, he felt at last that every misfortune that he could invent was lost in the depths of the real sorrow which oppressed his own life, and out of this knowledge came an idea for his ballad. What a fool never to have thought of it before!

He would write the history—the miserable bitter history—of a great man born to a small way of life, whose merits should raise him from his low estate to a deserved and glorious fame; who should toil, and strive, and struggle, and when his hopes and prayers seemed to be at last fulfilled, and the reward of his labours at hand, should awake and find that it was a dream; that he was no nearer to Fame than ever, and that he might never reach it. Here was enough sorrow for a tragedy. The ballad should be written now.

The next day. Friedrich plunged into the bookseller's shop.

"Well, now, what is it?" smiled the comfortable little bookseller.

"I want some paper, please," gasped Friedrich; "a good big bit if I may have it, and, if you please, I must go now. I will come and clean out the shop for you at the end of the week, but I am very busy to-day."

"The condition of the shop," said the little bookseller, grandiloquently, with a wave of his hand, "yields to more important matters; namely, to thy condition, my child, which is not of the best. Thou art as white as this sheet of paper, to which thou art heartily welcome. I am silent, but not ignorant. Thou wouldst be a writer, but art not yet a philosopher, my Friedrich. Thou art not fast-set on thy philosophic equilibrium. Thou hast knocked down three books and a stool since thou hast come in the shop. Be calm, my child: consider that even if truly also the fast-bound-eternally-immutable-condition of everlastingly-varying-circumstance—"

But by this time Friedrich was at home.

How he got through the next three days he never knew. He stumbled in and out of the house with the awkwardness of an idiot, and was so stupid in school that nothing but his previous good character saved him from a flogging. The day before the Feast of St. Nicholas (which was a holiday) the schoolmaster dismissed him with the severe inquiry, if he meant to be a dunce all his life? and Friedrich went home with two sentences ringing in his head—

"Do I mean to be a dunce all my life?"

"Friedrich can do nothing useful."

To-night the ballad must be finished.

He contrived to sit up beyond his usual hour, and escaped notice by crouching behind a large linen chest, and there wrote and wrote till his heart beat and his head felt as if it would split in pieces. At last, the careful mother discovered that Friedrich had not bid her good-night, and he was brought out of his hiding-place and sent to bed.

He took a light and went softly up the ladder into the loft, and, to his great satisfaction, found the others asleep. He said his prayers, and got into bed, but he did not put out the light; he put a box behind it to prevent its being seen, and drew out his paper and wrote. The ballad was done, but he must make a fair copy for the Maerchen-Frau; and very hard work it was, in his feverish excited state, to write out a thing that was finished. He worked resolutely, however, and at last completed it with trembling hands, and pushed it under his pillow.

Then he sat up in bed, and looked round him.

Time passed, and still he sat shivering and clasping his knees, and the reason he sat so was—because he dared not lie down.

The work was done, and the overstrained mind, no longer occupied, filled with ghastly fears and fancies. He did not dare to put out the light, and yet its faint glimmer only made the darkness more horrible. He did not dare to look behind him, though he knew that there was nothing there. He trembled at the scratching sound in the wainscot, though he knew that it was only mice. A sudden light on the window, and a distant chorus, did not make his heart beat less wildly from being nothing more alarming than two or three noisy students going home with torches. Then his light took the matter into its own hands, and first flared up with a suddenness that almost made Friedrich jump out of his skin, and then left him in total darkness. He could endure no longer, and, scrambling out of bed, crossed the floor to where the warm light came up the steps of the ladder from the room beneath. There our hero crouched without daring to move, and comforted himself with the sounds of life below. But it was very wearying, and yet he dared not go back. A neighbour had "dropped in," and he could see figures passing to and fro across the kitchen.

At last his sister passed, with the light shining on her golden plaits, and he risked a low murmur of "Marie! Marie!"

She stopped an instant, and then passed on; but after a few minutes, she returned, and came up the ladder with her finger on her lips to enjoin silence. He needed no caution, being instinctively aware that if one parental duty could be more obvious than another to the tradesman, it would be that of crushing such folly as Friedrich was displaying by timely severity. The boy crept back to bed, and Marie came after him.

There are unheroic moments in the lives of the greatest of men, and though when the head is strong and clear, and there is plenty of light and good company, it is highly satisfactory and proper to smile condescension upon female inanity, there are times when it is not unpleasant to be at the mercy of kind arms that pity without asking a reason, and in whose presence one may be foolish without shame. And it is not ill, perhaps, for some of us, whose acutely strung minds go up with every discovery, and down with every doubt, if we have some humble comforter (whether woman or man) on whose face a faithful spirit has set the seal of peace—a face which in its very steadfastness is "as the face of an angel."

Such a face looked down upon Friedrich, before which fancied horrors fled; and he wound his arms round Marie's neck, and laid down his head, and was comfortable, if not sublime.

After a dozen or so of purposeless kisses, she spoke—

"What is it, my beloved?"

"I—I don't think I can get to sleep," said the poet.

Marie abstained from commenting on this remark, and Friedrich was silent and comfortable. So comfortable that, though he despised her opinion on such matters he asked it in a low whisper—"Marie, dost thou not think it would be the very best thing in the world to be a great man? To labour and labour for it, and be a great man at last?"

Marie's answer was as low, but quite decided—

"No."

"Why not, Marie?"

"It is very nice to be great, and I should love to see thee a great man, Friedrich, very well indeed, but the very best thing of all is to be good. Great men are not always happy ones, though when they are good also it is very glorious, and makes one think of the words of the poor heathen in Lycaonia—'The gods have come down to us in the likeness of men.' But if ever thou art a great man, little brother, it will be the good and not the great things of thy life that will bring thee peace. Nay, rather, neither thy goodness nor thy greatness, but the mercy of GOD!"

And in this opinion Marie was obstinately fixed, and Friedrich argued no more.

"I think I shall do now," said the hero at last; "I thank thee very much, Marie."

She kissed him anew, and bade GOD bless him, and wished him good-night, and went down the ladder till her golden plaits caught again the glow of the warm kitchen, and Friedrich lost sight of her tall figure and fair face, and was alone once more.

He was better, but still he could not sleep. Wearied and vexed, he lay staring into the darkness till he heard steps upon the ladder, and became the involuntary witness of—the true St. Nicholas.

It was the mother, with a basket in her hand, and Friedrich watched her as she approached the place where all the shoes were laid out, his among them.

The children were by no means immaculate or in any way greatly superior to other families, but the mother was tender-hearted, and had a poor memory for sins that were past, and Friedrich saw her fill one shoe after another with cakes and sweetmeats. At last she came to his, and then she stopped. He lifted up his head, and an indefinable fury surged in his heart. He had been very tiresome since the ballad was begun; was she going to put rods into his shoes only? *His*! He could have borne anything but this. Meanwhile, she was fumbling in the basket; and, at last, pulled out—not a rod, but—a paper of cakes of another kind, to which Friedrich was particularly attached, and with these she lined the shoes thickly, and filled them up with sweetmeats, and passed on.

"Oh, mother! mother! Far, far too kind!" The awkwardness and stupidity of yesterday, and of many yesterdays, smote him to the heart, and roused once more the only too ready tears. But he did not cry long, he had a happy feeling of community with his brothers and sisters in getting more than they any of them deserved; to have seen the St. Nicholas's proceedings had diverted his mind from gloomy fancies, and altogether, with a comfortable sensation of cakes and kindness, he fell asleep smiling, and slept soundly and well.

The next day he threw his arms round his mother, and said

that the cakes were "so nice."

"But I don't deserve them," he added.

"Thou'lt mend," said she kindly. "And no doubt the Saint knew that thou hadst eaten but half a dinner for a week past, and brought those cakes to tempt thee; so eat them all, my child; for, doubtless, there are plenty more where they come from."

"I am very much obliged to whoever did think of it," said Friedrich.

"And plenty more there are," said the good woman to Marie afterwards, as they were dishing the dinner. "Luise Jansen's shop is full of them. But, bless the boy! he's too clever for anything. There's no playing St. Nicholas with him."

The day went by at last, and the evening came on. The tradesman went off of himself to see if he could meet with the Burgomaster, and the children became rabid in their impatience for Friedrich's ballad.

He would not read it himself, so Marie was pressed into the service, and crowned with the hood and cloak, and elected Maerchen-Frau.

The author himself sat in an arm-chair, with a face as white and miserable as if he were ordered for execution. He formed a painful contrast to his ruddy brothers and sisters; and it would seem as if he had begun already to experience the truth of Marie's assertion, that "great men are not always happy ones."

The ballad was put into the Maerchen-Frau's hands, and she was told that Friedrich had written it. She gave a quick glance at it, and asked if he had really invented it all. The children repeated the fact, which was a pleasant but not a surprising one to them, and Marie began.

The young poet had evidently a good ear, for the verses were easy and musical, and the metre more than tolerably correct; and as the hero of the ballad worked harder and harder, and got higher and higher, the children clapped their hands, and discovered that it was "quite like Friedrich."

Why, when that hero was almost at the height of fortune, and the others gloried in his success, did the foolish author bury his face upon his arms, and sob silently but bitterly in sympathy?—moreover, with such a heavy and absorbing grief that he did not hear it, when Marie stopped for an instant and then went on again, or know that steps had come behind his chair, and that his father and the Burgomaster were in the room.

The Maerchen-Frau went on; the hero awoke from his unreal happiness to his real fate, and bewailed in verse after verse the heavy weights of birth, and poverty, and circumstance, that kept him from the heights of fame. The ballad was ended.

Then a voice fell on Friedrich's ear, which nearly took away his breath. It was his father's asking sternly, "What is all this?"

And then he knew that Marie was standing up, with a strange emotion on her face, and he heard her say—

"It is a poem that Friedrich has written. He has written it all himself. Every word. And he is but twelve years old!" She was pointing to him, or, perhaps, the Burgomaster might not have recognized in that huddled miserable figure the genius of the family.

His was the next voice, and what he said Friedrich could hardly remember; the last sentences only he clearly understood.

"GOD has not blessed me with children, neighbour. My wife, as well as I, would be ashamed if such genius were lost for want of a little money. Give the child to me. He shall have a liberal education, and will be a great man."

"I shall not," said the tradesman, "stand in the way of his interests or your commands. I cannot tell what to say to your kindness, Burgomaster. GOD willing, I hope he will be a credit to the town."

"GOD willing, he will be a credit to his country," said the Burgomaster.

The words rang in Friedrich's ears over and over again, like the changes of bells. They danced before his eyes as if he saw them in a book. They were written in his heart as if "graven with an iron pen and lead in the rock for ever."

"GOD *willing, I hope he will be a credit to the town.*"

"GOD *willing, he will be a credit to his country.*"

"*He shall have a liberal education, and will be a* GREAT MAN."

Friedrich tried to stand on his feet and thank the Burgomaster; who, on any other occasion, might have been tempted to suppose him an idiot, so white and distorted was the child's face, struggling through tears and smiles. He could not utter a word; a mist began to come before his eyes, through which the Burgomaster's head seemed to bob up and down, and then his father's, and his mother's, and Marie's, with a look of pity on her face. He tried to tell *her* that he was now a great man and felt quite happy; but, unfortunately, was only able to burst into tears, and then to burst out laughing, and then a sharp pain shot through his head, and he remembered no more.

*　*　*　*　*

Friedrich had a dim consciousness of coming round after this, and being put to bed; then he fell asleep, and slept heavily. When he woke Marie was sitting by his side, and it was dark. The mother had gone downstairs, she said, and she had taken her place. Friedrich lay silent for a bit; at last he said,

"I am very happy, Marie."

"I am very glad, dearest."

"Dost thou think father will let the Burgomaster give me a good education, Marie?"

"Yes, dear, I am sure he will."

"It is very kind," said Friedrich, thoughtfully; "for I know he wants me for the business. But I will help him some day. And, Marie, I will be a good man, and when I am very rich I will give great alms to the poor."

"Thou wilt be a good man before thou art a rich one, I trust," said his dogmatic sister. "We are accepted in that we have, and not in that we have not. Thou hast great talent, and wilt give it to the Lord, whether He make thee rich or no. Wilt thou not, dearest?"

"What dost thou mean, Marie? Am I never to write anything but hymns?"

"No, no, I do not mean that," she said. "I am very ignorant and cannot rightly explain it to thee, little brother. But genius is a great and perilous gift; and, oh, Friedrich! Friedrich! promise me just this:—that thou wilt never, never write anything against the faith or the teaching of the Saviour, and that thou wilt never use the graces of poetry to cover the hideousness of any of those sins which it is the work of a lifetime to see justly, and to fight against manfully. Promise me just this."

"Oh, Marie! to think that I could be so wicked!"

"No! no!" she said, covering him with kisses. "I know thou wilt be good and great, and we shall all be proud of our little brother. GOD give thee the pen of a ready writer, and grace to use it to His glory!"

"I will," he said, "GOD help me! and I will write beautiful hymns for thee, Marie, that when I am dead shall be sung in the churches. They shall be like that Evening Hymn we sing so often. Sing it now, my sister!"

Marie cleared her throat, and in a low voice, that steadied and grew louder and sweeter till it filled the house and died away among the rafters, sang the beautiful hymn that begins—

"Herr, Dein Auge geht nicht unter, wenn es bei uns Abend wird;" (Lord! Thine eye does not go down, when it is evening with us.)

The boy lay drinking it in with that full enjoyment of simple vocal music which is so innate in the German character; and as he lay, he hummed his accustomed part in it, and the mother at work below caught up the song involuntarily, and sang at her work; and Marie's clear voice breaking through the wooden walls of the house, was heard by a passer in the street, who struck in with the bass of the familiar hymn, and went his way. Before it was ended, Friedrich was sleeping peacefully once more.

But Marie sat by the stove till the watchman in the quaint old street told the hour of midnight, when (with the childish custom taught her by the old schoolmaster long ago) she folded her hands, and murmured,

> "Nisi Dominus urbem custodiat, frustra vigilat custos." (Except the Lord keep the city, the watchman waketh but in vain.)

And then she slept also.

The snow fell softly on the roof, and on the walls of the old church outside, and on the pavement of the street of the poet's native town, and the night passed and the day came.

There is little more to tell, for that night was the last night of his sorrowful humble childhood, and that day was the first day of his fame.

*   *   *   *   *

The Duke of—was an enlightened and generous man, and a munificent patron of the Arts and Sciences, and of literary and scientific men. He was not exactly a genius, but he was highly accomplished. He wrote a little, and played a little, and drew a little; and with fortune to befriend him, as a natural consequence he published a little, and composed a little, and framed his pictures.

But what was better and more remarkable than this, was the generous spirit in which he loved and admired those who did great things in the particular directions in which he did a little. He bought good pictures while he painted bad ones; and those writers, musicians, and artists who could say but little for his performances, had every reason to talk loudly of his liberality. He was the special admirer of talent born in obscurity; and at the time of which we are writing (many years after the events related above), the favourite "lion" in the literary clique he had gathered round him in his palace, was a certain poet—the son of a small tradesman in a small town, who had been educated by the kindness of the Burgomaster (long dead), and who now had made Germany to ring with his fame; who had visited the Courts of Europe, and received compliments from Royalty, whose plays were acted in the theatres, whose poems stood on the shelves of the booksellers, who was a great man—Friedrich!

It was a lovely evening, and the Duke, leaning on the arm of his favourite, walked up and down a terrace. The Duke was (as usual) in the best possible humour. The poet (as was not uncommon) was just in the slightest degree inclined to be in a bad one. They had been reading a critique on his poems. It was praise, it is true, but the praise was not judiciously administered, and the poet was aggrieved. He rather felt (as authors are not unapt to feel) that a poet who could write such poems should have critics created with express capabilities for understanding him. But the good Duke was in his most cheery and amiable mood, and quite bent upon smoothing his ruffled lion into the same condition.

"What impossible creatures you geniuses are to please!" he said. "Tell me, my friend, has there ever been, since you first began your career, a bit of homage or approbation that has really pleased you?"

"Oh, yes!" said the poet, in a tone that sounded like Oh, no!

"I don't believe it," said the Duke. "Come, now, could you, if you were asked, describe the happiest and proudest hour of your life?"

A new expression came into the poet's eyes, and lighted up his gaunt intellectual face. Some old memories awoke within him, and it is doubtful if he saw the landscape at which he was gazing. But the Duke was not quick, though kind; he thought that Friedrich had not heard him, and repeated the question.

"Yes," said the poet. "Yes, indeed I could."

"Well, then, let me guess," said the Duke, facetiously. (He fancied that he was bringing his crusty genius into capital condition.) "Was it when your great tragedy of 'Boadicea' was first performed in Berlin, and the theatre rose like one man to offer homage, and the gods sent thunder? I wish they had ever treated my humble efforts with as much favour. Was it then?"

"No!"

"Was it when his Imperial Majesty the Emperor of—was pleased to present you with a gold snuff-box set with diamonds, and to express his opinion that your historical plays were incomparably among the finest productions of poetic genius?"

"His Imperial Majesty," said Friedrich, "is a brave soldier; but, a—hem!—an indifferent critic. I do not take snuff, and his Imperial Majesty does not read poetry. The interview was gratifying, but that was not the occasion. No!"

"Was it when you were staying with Dr. Kranz at G—, and the students made that great supper for you, and escorted your carriage both ways with a procession of torches?"

"Poor boys!" said the poet, laughing; "it was very kind, and they could ill afford it. But they would have drunk quite as much wine for any one who would have taken the inside out of the University clock, or burnt the Principal's wig, as they did for me. It was a very unsteady procession that brought me home, I assure you. The way they poked the torches in each other's faces left one student, as I heard, with no less than eight duels on his hands. And, oh! the manner in which they howled my most pathetic love songs! No! no!"

The Duke laughed heartily.

"Is it any of the various occasions on which the fair ladies of Germany have testified their admiration by offerings of sympathy and handiwork?"

"No!" roared the poet.

"Are you quite sure?" said the Duke, slyly. "I have heard of comforters, and slippers, and bouquets, and locks of hair, besides a dozen of warm stockings knit by the fair hands of—"

"Spare me!" groaned Friedrich, in mock indignation. "Am I a pet preacher, that I should be smothered in female absurdities? I have hair that would stuff a sofa, comforters that would protect a regiment in Siberia, slippers, stockings—. I shall sell them, I shall burn them. I would send them back, but the ladies send nothing but their Christian names, and to identify Luise, and Gretchen, and Catherine, and Bettina, is beyond my powers. No!"

Juliana Horatia Ewing

When they had ceased laughing the Duke continued his catechism.

"Was it when the great poet G—(your only rival) paid that handsome compliment to your verses on—"

"No!" interrupted the poet. "A thousand times no! The great poet praised the verses you allude to simply to cover his depreciation of my 'Captive Queen,' which is among my best efforts, but too much in his own style. How Germany can worship his bombastic—but that's nothing! No."

"Was it when you passed accidentally through the streets of Dresden, and the crowd discovered you, and carried you to the hotel on its shoulders?"

The momentary frown passed from Friedrich's face, and he laughed again.

"And when the men who carried me twisted my leg so that I couldn't walk for a fortnight, to say nothing of the headache I endured from bowing to the populace like a Chinese mandarin? No!"

"Is it any triumph you have enjoyed in any other country in Europe?"

"No!"

"My dear genius, I can guess no more; what, in the name of Fortune, was this happy occasion—this life triumph?"

"It is a long story, your highness, and entertaining to no one but myself."

"You do me injustice," said the Duke. "A long story from

you is too good to be lost. Sit down, and favour me."

A patron's wishes are not to be neglected; and somewhat unwillingly the poet at last sat down, and told the story of his Ballad and of St. Nicholas's Day, as it has been told here. The fountain of tears is drier in middle age than in childhood, but he was not unmoved as he concluded.

"Every circumstance of that evening," he said, "is as fresh in my remembrance now as it was then, and will be till I die. It is a joy, a triumph, and a satisfaction that will never fade. The words that roused me from despair, that promised knowledge to my ignorance and fame to my humble condition, have power now to make my heart beat, and to bring hopeful tears into eyes that should have dried with age—

"GOD *willing, he will be a credit to the town.*"

"GOD *willing, he will be a credit to his country.*"

"*He shall have a liberal education, and will be a great man.*"

"It is as good as a poem," said the delighted Duke. "I shall tell the company to-night that I am the most fortunate man in Germany. I have heard your unpublished poem. By the bye, Poet, is that ballad published?"

"No, and never will be. It shall never know less kindly criticism than it received then."

"And are you really in earnest? Was this indeed the happiest triumph your talents have ever earned?"

"It was," said Friedrich. "The first blast on the trumpet of Fame is the sweetest. Afterwards, we find it out of tune."

"Your parents are dead, I think?"

"They are, and so is my youngest sister."

"And what of Marie?"

"She married—a man who, I think, is in no way worthy of her. Not a bad, but a stupid man, with strong Bible convictions on the subject of marital authority. She is such an angel in his house as he can never understand in this world."

"Do you ever see her?"

"Sometimes, when I want a rest. I went to see her not long ago, and found her just the same as ever. I sat at her feet, and laid my head in her lap, and tried to be a child again. I bade her tell me the history of Bluebeard, and strove to forget that I had ever lost the childish simplicity which she has kept so well;—and I almost succeeded. I had forgotten that the great poet was jealous of my 'Captive Queen,' and told myself it would be a grand thing to be like him. I thought I should like to see a live Emperor. But just when the delusion was perfect, there was a row in the street. The people had found me out, and I must show myself at the window. The spell was broken. I have not tried it again."

They were on the steps of the palace.

"Your story has entertained and touched me beyond measure," said the Duke. "But something is wanting. It does not (as they say) 'end well.' I fear you are not happy."

"I am content," said Friedrich. "Yes, I am happy. I never could be a child again, even if it pleased GOD to restore to me the circumstances of my childhood. It is best as it is, but I have learnt the truth of what Marie told me. It is the good, and not the great things of my life that bring me peace; or rather, neither one nor the other, but the undeserved mercies of my GOD!"

*   *   *   *   *

For those who desire to know more of the poet's life than has been told, this is added. He did not live to be very old. A painful disease (the result of mental toil), borne through many years, ended his life almost in its prime. He retained his faculties till the last, and bore protracted suffering with a heroism and endurance which he had not always displayed in smaller trials. The medical men pronounced, on the authority of a *post-mortem* examination, that he must for years have suffered a silent martyrdom. Truly, his bodily sufferings (when known at last) might well excuse many weaknesses and much moody, irritable impatience; especially when it is remembered that the mental sufferings of intellectual men are generally great in proportion to their gifts, and (when clogged with nerves and body that are ever urged beyond their strength) that they often mock the pride of humanity by leaving but little space between the genius and the madman.

Another fact was not known till he had died—his charity. Then it was discovered how much kindness he had exercised in secret, and that three poor widows had been fed daily from his table during all the best years of his prosperity. Before his death he arranged all his affairs, even to the disposal of his worn-out body.

"My country has been gracious to me," he said, "and, if it cares, may dispose of my carcase as it will. But I desire that after my death my heart may be taken from my body and buried at the feet of my father and my mother in the churchyard of my native town. At their feet," he added, with some of the old imperiousness—"strong in death." "At their feet, remember!"

In one of the largest cities of Germany, a huge marble monument is erected to the memory of the Great Man. On three sides of the pedestal are bas-relief designs illustrating some of his works, whereby three fellow-countrymen added to their fame; and on the fourth is a fine inscription in Latin, setting forth his talents, and his virtues, and the honours conferred on him, and stating in conclusion (on the authority of his eulogizer) that his works have gained for him immortality.

In a quiet green churchyard, near a quiet little town, under the shadow of the quaint old church, a little cross marks the graves of a tradesman and of his wife who lived and laboured in their generation, and are at rest. Near them, daisies grow above the dust of the "Fraeulein," which awaits the resurrection from the dead. And at the feet of that simple couple lies the heart of their great son—a heart which the sickness of earthly hope and the fever of earthly ambition shall disturb no more.

By the Poet's own desire, "the rude memorial" that marks the spot contains no more than his initials, and a few words in his native tongue to mark the foundation of the only ambition that he could feel in death—

"Ich verlasse mich auf Gottes Guete immer und ewiglich."

—*My trust is in the tender mercy of* GOD *for ever and ever.*

A BIT OF GREEN

"Thou oughtest, therefore, to call to mind the more heavy sufferings of others, that so thou mayest the easier bear thy own very small troubles."

—THE IMITATION OF CHRIST

Children who live always with grass and flowers at their feet, and a clear sky overhead, can have no real idea of the charm that country sights and sounds have for those whose home is in a dirty, busy, manufacturing town—just such a town, in fact, as I lived in when I was a boy, which is more than twenty years ago.

My father was a doctor, with a very large, if not what is called a "genteel," practice, and we lived in a comfortable house in a broad street. I was born and bred there; and, ever since I could remember, the last sound that soothed my ears at night, and the first to which I awoke in the morning, was the eternal rumbling and rattling of the carts and carriages as they passed over the rough stones. I never noticed if I heard them in the day-time, but at night my chief amusement, as I lay in bed, was to guess by the sound of the wheels what sort of vehicle was passing.

Juliana Horatia Ewing

"That light sharp rattle is a cab," I thought. "What a noise it makes, and gone in a moment! One gentleman inside, I should think. There's an omnibus; and there, jolty-jolt, goes a light cart; that's a carriage, by the way the horses step; and now, rumbling heavily in the distance, and coming slowly nearer, and heavier, and louder, this can be nothing but a brewer's dray!" And the dray came so slowly that I was asleep before it had got safely out of hearing.

Ours was a very noisy street, but the noise made the night cheerful; and so did the church clock near, which struck the quarters; and so did the light of the street lamps, which came through the blind and fell upon my little bed. We had very little light, except gaslight and daylight, in our street; the sunshine seldom found its way to us, and, when it did, people were so little used to it that they pulled down the blinds for fear it should hurt the carpets. In the room my sister and I called our nursery, however, we always welcomed it with blinds rolled up to the very top; and, as we had no carpet, no damage was done.

But sunshine outside will not always make sunshine shine within, and I remember one day when, though our nursery was unusually cheerful, and though the windows were reflected in square patches of sunlight on the floor, I stood in the very midst of the brightness, grumbling and kicking at my sister's chair with a face as black as a thunder-cloud. The reason of my ill-temper was this: Ever since I could remember, my father had been accustomed, once a year, to take us all into the country for change of air. Once he had taken us to the sea, but generally we went to an old farmhouse in the middle of the beautiful moors which lay not many miles from our dirty black town. But this year, on this very sunshiny morning, he had announced at breakfast that he could not let us go to what we called our moor-home. He had even added insult to injury by expressing his thankfulness that we were all in good health, so that the change was not a matter of necessity. I was too indignant to speak, and rushed upstairs into the nursery, where my little sister had also taken refuge. She was always very gentle and obedient (provokingly so, I thought), and now she sat rocking her doll on her knee in silent sorrow, whilst I stood kicking her chair and grumbling in a tone which it was well the doll could not hear, or rocking would have been of little use. I took pleasure in trying to make her as angry as myself. I reminded her how lovely the purple moors were looking at that moment, how sweet heather smelt, and how good bilberries tasted. I said I thought it was "very hard." It wasn't as if we were always paying visits, as many children did, to their country relations; we had only one treat in the year, and father wanted to take that away. Not a soul in the town, I said, would be as unfortunate as we were. The children next door would go somewhere, of course. So would the little Smiths, and the Browns, and *everybody*. Everybody else went to the sea in the autumn; we were contented with the moors, and he wouldn't even let us go there. And, at the end of every burst of complaint, I discharged a volley of kicks at the leg of the chair, and wound up with "I can't think why he can't!"

"I don't know," said my sister, timidly, "but he said something about not affording it, and spending money, and about trade being bad, and he was afraid there would be great distress in the town."

Oh, these illogical women! I was furious. "What on earth has that to do with us?" I shouted at her. "Father's a doctor; trade won't hurt him. But you are so silly, Minnie, I can't talk to you. I only know it's very hard. Fancy staying a whole year boxed up in this beastly town!" And I had so worked myself up that I fully believed in the truth of the sentence with which I concluded—

"*There never* WAS *anything so miserable!*"

Minnie said nothing, for my feelings just then were something like those of the dogs who (Dr. Watts tells us)

"delight
To bark and bite;"

and perhaps she was afraid of being bitten. At any rate, she held her tongue; and just then my father came into the room.

The door was open, and he must have heard my last speech as he came along the passage; but he made no remark on it, and only said, "Would any young man here like to go with me to see a patient?"

I went willingly, for I was both tired and half-ashamed of teasing Minnie, and we were soon in the street. It was a broad and cheerful one, as I said; but before long we left it for a narrower, and then turned off from that into a side street, where the foot-path would only allow us to walk in single file—a dirty, dark lane, where surely the sun never did shine.

"What a horrid place!" I said. "I never was here before. Why don't they pull such a street down?"

"What is to become of the people who live in it?" said my father.

"Let them live in one of the bigger streets," I said; "it would be much more comfortable."

"Very likely," he said; "but they would have to pay much more for their houses; and if they haven't the money to pay with, what's to be done?"

I could not say, for, like older social reformers than myself, I felt more sure that the reform was needed, than of how to accomplish it. But before I could decide upon what to do with the dirty little street, we had come to a place so very much worse that it put the other quite out of my head. There is a mournful fatality about the pretty names which are given, as if in mockery, to the most wretched of the bye-streets in large towns. The street we had left was called Rosemary Street, and this was Primrose Place.

Primrose Place was more like a yard than a street; the houses were all irregular and of different ages. On one side was a gap with palings round it, where building was going on, and beyond rose a huge black factory. But the condition of Primrose Place was beyond description. I had never seen anything like it before, and kept as close to my father as was consistent with boyish, dignity. The pathway was broken up, children squalled at the doors and quarrelled in the street, which was strewn with rags, and bones, and bits of old iron, and shoes, and the tops of turnips. I do not think there was a whole unbroken window in all the row of tall miserable houses, and the wet clothes hanging out on lines stretched across the street, flapped above our heads. I counted three cripples as we went up Primrose Place. My father stopped to speak to several people, and I heard many complaints of the bad state of trade to which my sister had alluded. He gave some money to one woman, and spoke kindly to all; but he hurried me on as fast as he could, and we turned at last into one of the houses.

My ill-humour had by this time almost worked itself off in the fresh air, and the novel scenes through which we had come; and, for the present, the morning's disappointment was forgotten as I followed my father through the crowded miserable rooms, and clambered up staircase after staircase, till we reached the top of the house, and stumbled through a latched door into the garret. After so much groping in the dark, the light dazzled me, and I thought at first that the room was empty. But at last a faint "Good day" from the corner near the window drew my eyes that way; and there, stretched on a sort of bed, and supported by a chair at his back, lay the patient we had come to see.

He was a young man about twenty-six years old, in the last stage of that terrible disease so fatally common in our country—he was dying of consumption. There was no mistaking the flushed cheek, the painfully laborious breathing, and the incessant cough; while two old crutches in the corner spoke of another affliction—he was a cripple. His gaunt face lighted up with a glow of pleasure when my father came in, who seated himself at once on the end of the bed, and began to talk to him, whilst I looked round the room. There was absolutely nothing in it, except the bed on which the sick man lay, the chair that supported him, and a small three-legged table. The low roof was terribly out of repair, and the window was patched with newspaper; but through the glass panes that were left, in full glory streamed the sun, and in the midst of the blaze stood a pot of musk in full bloom. The soft yellow flowers looked so grand, and smelled so sweet, that I was lost in admiration, till I found the sick man's black eyes fixed on mine.

"You are looking at my bit of green, master?" he said, in a gratified tone.

"Do you like flowers?" I inquired, coming shyly up to the bed.

"Do I like 'em?" he exclaimed in a low voice. "Ay, I love 'em well enough—well enough," and he looked fondly at the plant, "though it's long since I saw any but these."

"You have not been in the country for a long time?" I

inquired, compassionately. I felt sad to think that he had perhaps lain there for months, without a taste of fresh air or a run in the fields; but I was *not* prepared for his answer.

"*I never was in the country, young gentleman.*"

I looked at my father.

"Yes," he said, in answer to my glance, "it is quite true. William was born here. He got hurt when a boy, and has been lame ever since. For some years he has been entirely confined to the house. He was never out of town, and never saw a green field."

Never out of the town! confined to the house for years! and what a house! The tears rushed to my eyes, and I felt that angry heart-ache which the sight of suffering produces in those who are too young to be insensible to it, and too ignorant of GOD's Providence to submit with "quietness and confidence" to His will.

"My son can hardly believe it, William."

"It is such a shame," I said; "it is horrible. I am very sorry for you."

The black eyes turned kindly upon me, and the sick man said, "Thank you heartily, Sir. You mean very kindly. I used to say the same sort of things myself, when I was younger, and knew no better. I used to think it was very hard, and that no one was so miserable as I was. But I know now how much better off I am than most folks, and how many things I have to be thankful for."

I looked round the room, and began involuntarily to count the furniture—one, two, three. The "many things" were certainly not chairs and tables.

But he was gazing before him, and went on: "I often think how thankful I ought to be to die in peace, and have a quiet room to myself. There was a girl in a consumption on the floor below me; and she used to sit and cough, while her father and mother quarrelled so that I could hear them through the floor. I used to send her half of anything nice I had, but I found they took it. I did wish then," he added, with a sudden flush, "that I had been a strong man!"

"How shocking!" I said.

"Yes," he answered; "it was that first set me thinking how many mercies I had. And then there came such a good parson to St. John's, and he taught me many things; and then I knew your father; and the neighbours have been very kind. And while I could work I got good wage, and laid by a bit; and I've sold a few things, and there'll be these to sell when I'm gone; and so I've got what will keep me while I do live, and pay for my coffin. What can a man want more?"

What, indeed! Unsatisfied heart, make answer!

A fit of coughing that shook the crazy room interrupted him here. When he had recovered himself, he turned to my father.

"Ay, ay, I have many mercies, as you know, Sir. Who would have thought I could have kept a bit of green like that plant of mine in a place like this? But, you see, they pulled down those old houses opposite just before I got it, and now the sun couldn't come into a king's room better than it comes into mine. I was always afraid, year after year, that they would build it up, and my bit of green would die; and they are building now, but it will last my time. Indeed, indeed, I've had much to be thankful for. Not," he added, in a low, reverential tone, "not to mention greater blessings. The presence of the LORD! the presence of the LORD!"

I was awed, almost frightened, by the tone in which he spoke, and by the look of his face, on which the shadow of death was falling fast. He lay in a sort of stupor, gazing with his black eyes at the broken roof, as if through it he saw something invisible to us.

It was some time before he seemed to recollect that we were there, and before I ventured to ask him. "Where did you get your plant?"

He smiled. "That's a long story, master; but it was this way. You see, my father died quite young in a decline, and left my mother to struggle on with eight of us as she could. She buried six, one after another; and then she died herself, and brother Ben and I were left alone. But we were mighty fond of one another, and got on very well. I got plenty of employment, weaving mats and baskets for a shop in the town, and Ben worked at the factory. One Saturday night he came home all in a state, and said there was going to be a cheap trip on the Monday into the country. It was the first there had been from these parts, though there have been many since, I believe. Neither he nor I had ever been out of the town, and he was full of it that we must go. He had brought his Saturday wage with him, and we would work hard afterwards. Well, you see, the landlord had been that day, and had said he must have the rent by Tuesday, or he'd turn us out. I'd got some of it laid by, and was looking to Ben's wages to make it up. But I couldn't bear to see his face pining for a bit of fresh air, and so I thought I could stay at home and work on Monday for what would make up the rent, and he need never know. So I pretended that I didn't want to go, and couldn't be bothered with the fuss; and at last I set him off on Monday without me. It was late at night when he came back like one wild. He'd got flowers in his hat, and flowers in all his button-holes; he'd got his handkerchief filled with hay, and was carrying something under his coat. He began laughing and crying, and 'Eh, Bill!' he said, 'thou hast been a fool. Thou hast missed summat. But I've brought thee a bit of green, lad, I've brought thee a bit of green.' And then he lifted up his coat, and there was the plant, which some woman had given him. We didn't sleep much that night. He spread the hay over the bed, for me to lay my face on, and see how the fields smelt, and then he began and told me all about it; and after that, when I was tired with work, or on a Sunday afternoon, I used to say, 'Now, Ben, tell us a bit about the country.' And he liked nothing better. He used to say that I should go, if he carried me on his back; but the LORD did not see fit. He took cold at work, and went off three months afterwards. It was singular, the morning he died he called me to him, and said, 'Bill, I've been a dreaming about that trip that thou didst want to go after all. I dreamt—' and then he stopped, and said no more; but, after a bit, he opened his eyes wide, and pulled me to him, and he said, 'Bill, my lad, there's such flowers in heaven, such flowers!' And so the LORD took him. But I kept the bit of green for his sake."

Here followed another fit of coughing, which brought my father from the end of the bed to forbid his talking any more.

"I have got to see another patient in the yard," he said, "and I will leave my son here. He shall read you a chapter or two till I come back; he is a good reader for his age."

And so my father went. I was, as he said, a good reader for my age; but I felt very nervous when the sick man drew a Bible from his side, and put it in my hands. I wondered what I should read; but it was soon settled by his asking for certain Psalms, which I read as clearly and distinctly as I could. At first I was rather disturbed by his occasional remarks, and a few murmured Amens; but I soon got used to it. He joined devoutly in the "Glory be to the Father"—with which I concluded—and then asked for a chapter from the Revelation of St. John. I was more at ease now, and read my best, with a happy sense of being useful; whilst he lay in the sunshine, folding the sheet with his bony fingers, with his eyes fixed on the beloved "bit of green," and drinking in the Words of Life with dying ears.

"Blessed are they that dwell in the heavenly Jerusalem, where there is no need of the sun, neither of the moon, to shine in it; for the glory of GOD *does lighten it, and the Lamb is the light thereof."*

By the time that my father returned, the sick man and I were fast friends; and I left him with his blessing on my head. As we went home, my good kind father told me that I was nearly old enough now to take an interest in his concerns, and began to talk of his patients, and of the poverty and destitution of some parts of the town. Then he spoke of the bad state of trade—that it was expected to be worse, and that the want of work and consequent misery this year would probably be very great. Finally he added, that when so many were likely to be starving, he had thought it right that we should deny ourselves our little annual treat, and so save the money to enable us to take our part in relieving the distressed.

"Don't you think so, my boy?" he concluded, as we reached the door of our comfortable (how comfortable!) home.

My whole heart was in my "Yes."

It is a happy moment for a son when his father first confides in him. It is a happy moment for a father when his son first learns to appreciate some of the labour of his life, and henceforth to obey his commands, not only with a blind obedience, but in the sympathizing spirit of the "perfect love" which "casts out fear." My heart was too full to thank him then for his wise forbearance and wiser confidence; but when after some months my sister's health made change of air to the house of a country relative necessary, great was my pride and thankfulness that I was well enough to remain at the post of duty by my father's side.

One day, not long after our visit to William, he went again to see him; and when he came back I saw by the musk-plant in his hand the news he brought. Its flowers were lovelier than ever, but its master was transplanted into a heavenly garden, and he had left it to me.

Mortal man does not learn any virtue in one lesson; and I have only too often in my life been ungrateful both to GOD and man. But the memory of lame William has often come across me when I have been tempted to grumble about small troubles; and has given me a little help (not to be despised) in striving after the grace of Thankfulness, even for a "bit of green."

MONSIEUR THE VISCOUNT'S FRIEND

A TALE IN THREE CHAPTERS

"Sweet are the vses of aduersitie
Which like the toad, ougly and venemous,
Weares yet a precious Iewell in his head."

—AS YOU LIKE IT: A.D. 1623.

CHAPTER I

It was the year of grace 1779. In one of the most beautiful corners of beautiful France stood a grand old chateau. It was a fine old building, with countless windows large and small, with high-pitched roofs and pointed towers, which in good taste or bad, did its best to be everywhere ornamental, from the gorgon heads which frowned from its turrets to the long row of stables and the fantastic dovecotes. It stood (as became such a castle) upon an eminence, and looked down. Very beautiful indeed was what it looked upon. Terrace below terrace glowed with the most brilliant flowers, and broad flights of steps led from one garden to the other. On the last terrace of all, fountains and jets of water poured into one large basin, in which were gold and silver fish. Beyond

Juliana Horatia Ewing

this were shady walks, which led to a lake on which floated water-lilies and swans. From the top of the topmost flight of steps you could see the blazing gardens one below the other, the fountains and the basin, the walks and the lake, and beyond these the trees, and the smiling country, and the blue sky of France.

Within the castle, as without, beauty reigned supreme. The sunlight, subdued by blinds and curtains, stole into rooms furnished with every grace and luxury that could be procured in a country that then accounted itself the most highly-civilized in the world. It fell upon beautiful flowers and beautiful china, upon beautiful tapestry and pictures; and it fell upon Madame the Viscountess, sitting at her embroidery. Madame the Viscountess was not young, but she was not the least beautiful object in those stately rooms. She had married into a race of nobles who (themselves famed for personal beauty) had been scrupulous in the choice of lovely wives. The late Viscount (for Madame was a widow) had been one of the handsomest of the gay courtiers of his day; and Madame had not been unworthy of him. Even now, though the roses on her cheeks were more entirely artificial than they had been in the days of her youth, she was like some exquisite piece of porcelain. Standing by the embroidery frame was Madame's only child, a boy who, in spite of his youth, was already Monsieur the Viscount. He also was beautiful. His exquisitely-cut mouth had a curl which was the inheritance of scornful generations, but which was redeemed by his soft violet eyes and by an under-lying expression of natural amiability. His hair was cut square across the forehead, and fell in natural curls behind. His childish figure had already been trained in the fencing school, and had gathered dignity from perpetually treading upon shallow steps and in lofty rooms. From the rosettes on his little shoes to his *chapeau a plumes*, he also was like some porcelain figure. Surely, such beings could not exist except in such a chateau as this, where the very air (unlike that breathed by common mortals) had in the ante-rooms a faint aristocratic odour, and was for yards round Madame the Viscountess dimly suggestive of frangipani!

Monsieur the Viscount did not stay long by the embroidery frame; he was entertaining to-day a party of children from the estate, and had come for the key of an old cabinet of which he wished to display the treasures. When tired of this, they went out on to the terrace, and one of the children who had not been there before exclaimed at the beauty of the view.

"It is true," said the little Viscount, carelessly, "and all, as far as you can see, is the estate."

"I will throw a stone to the end of your property, Monsieur," said one of the boys, laughing; and he picked one off the walk, and stepping back, flung it with all his little strength. The stone fell before it had passed the fountains, and the failure was received with shouts of laughter.

"Let us see who can beat that," they cried; and there was a general search for pebbles, which were flung at random among the flower beds.

"One may easily throw such as those," said the Viscount, who was poking under the wall of the first terrace; "but here is a stone that one may call a stone. Who will send this into the fish-pond? It will make a fountain of itself."

The children drew round him as, with ruffles turned back, he tugged and pulled at a large dirty looking stone, which was half-buried in the earth by the wall. "Up it comes!" said the Viscount, at length; and sure enough, up it came; but underneath it, his bright eyes shining out of his dirty wrinkled

Juliana Horatia Ewing

body—horror of horrors!—there lay a toad. Now, even in England, toads are not looked upon with much favour, and a party of English children would have been startled by such a discovery. But with French people, the dread of toads is ludicrous in its intensity. In France toads are believed to have teeth, to bite, and to spit poison; so my hero and his young guests must be excused for taking flight at once with a cry of dismay. On the next terrace, however, they paused, and seeing no signs of the enemy, crept slowly back again. The little Viscount (be it said) began to feel ashamed of himself, and led the way, with his hand upon the miniature sword which hung at his side. All eyes were fixed upon the fatal stone, when from behind it was seen slowly to push forth, first a dirty wrinkled leg, then half a dirty wrinkled head, with one gleaming eye. It was too much; with cries of, "It is he! he comes! he spits! he pursues us!" the young guests of the chateau fled in good earnest, and never stopped until they reached the fountain and the fish-pond.

But Monsieur the Viscount stood his ground. At the sudden apparition the blood rushed to his heart, and made him very white, then it flooded back again and made him very red, and then he fairly drew his sword, and shouting, "*Vive la France!*" rushed upon the enemy. The sword if small was sharp, and stabbed the poor toad would most undoubtedly have been, but for a sudden check received by the valiant little nobleman. It came in the shape of a large heavy hand that seized Monsieur the Viscount with the grasp of a giant, while a voice which could only have belonged to the owner of such a hand said in slow deep tones,

"*Que faites-vous?*" ("What are you doing?")

It was the tutor, who had been pacing up and down the terrace with a book, and who now stood holding the book in his right hand, and our hero in his left.

Monsieur the Viscount's tutor was a remarkable man. If he had not been so, he would hardly have been tolerated at the chateau, since he was not particularly beautiful, and not especially refined. He was in holy orders, as his tonsured head and clerical costume bore witness—a costume which, from its tightness and simplicity, only served to exaggerate the unusual proportions of his person. Monsieur the Preceptor had English blood in his veins, and his northern origin betrayed itself in his towering height and corresponding breadth, as well as by his fair hair and light blue eyes. But the most remarkable parts of his outward man were his hands, which were of immense size, especially about the thumbs. Monsieur the Preceptor was not exactly in keeping with his present abode. It was not only that he was wanting in the grace and beauty that reigned around him, but that his presence made those very graces and beauties to look small. He seemed to have a gift the reverse of that bestowed upon King Midas—the gold on which his heavy hand was laid seemed to become rubbish. In the presence of the late Viscount, and in that of Madame his widow, you would have felt fully the deep importance of your dress being *a la mode*, and your complexion *a la* strawberries and cream (such influences still exist); but let the burly tutor appear upon the scene, and all the magic died at once out of brocaded silks and pearl-coloured stockings, and dress and complexion became subjects almost of insignificance. Monsieur the Preceptor was certainly a singular man to have been chosen as an inmate of such a household; but, though young, he had unusual talents, and added to them the not more usual accompaniments of modesty and trustworthiness. To crown all, he was rigidly pious in times when piety was not fashionable, and an obedient son of the church of which he was a minister. Moreover, a family that fashion does not permit to be demonstratively religious, may gain a reflected credit from an austere chaplain; and so Monsieur the Preceptor remained in the chateau and went his own way. It was this man who now laid hands on the Viscount, and, in a voice that sounded like amiable thunder, made the inquiry, "*Que faites-vous?*"

"I am going to kill this animal—this hideous horrible animal," said Monsieur the Viscount, struggling vainly under the grasp of the tutors finger and thumb.

"It is only a toad," said Monsieur the Preceptor, in his laconic tones.

"*Only* a toad, do you say, Monsieur?" said the Viscount. "That is enough, I think. It will bite—it will spit—it will poison: it is like that dragon you tell me of, that devastated Rhodes—I am the good knight that shall kill it."

Monsieur the Preceptor laughed heartily. "You are misled by a vulgar error. Toads do not bite—they have no teeth; neither do they spit poison."

"You are wrong, Monsieur," said the Viscount; "I have seen their teeth myself. Claude Mignon, at the lodge, has two terrible ones, which he keeps in his pocket as a charm."

"I have seen them," said the tutor, "in Monsieur Claude's pocket. When he can show me similar ones in a toad's head I will believe. Meanwhile, I must beg of you, Monsieur, to put up your sword. You must not kill this poor animal, which is quite harmless, and very useful in a garden—it feeds upon many insects and reptiles which injure the plants."

"It shall not be useful, in this garden," said the little Viscount, fretfully. "There are plenty of gardeners to destroy the insects, and, if needful, we can have more. But the toad shall not remain. My mother would faint if she saw so hideous a beast among her beautiful flowers."

"Jacques!" roared the tutor to a gardener who was at some distance. Jacques started as if a clap of thunder had sounded in his ear, and approached with low bows. "Take that toad, Jacques, and carry it to the *potager*. It will keep the slugs from your cabbages."

Jacques bowed low and lower, and scratched his head, and then did reverence again with Asiatic humility, but at the same time moved gradually backwards, and never even looked at the toad.

"You also have seen the contents of Monsieur Claude's pocket?" said the tutor, significantly, and quitting his hold of the Viscount, he stooped down, seized the toad in his huge finger and thumb, and strode off in the direction of the *potager*, followed at a respectful distance by Jacques, who vented his awe and astonishment in alternate bows and exclamations at the astounding conduct of the incomprehensible Preceptor.

"What is the use of such ugly beasts?" said the Viscount to his tutor, on his return from the *potager*. "Birds and butterflies are pretty, but what can such villains as these toads have been made for?"

"You should study natural history, Monsieur—" began the priest, who was himself a naturalist.

"That is what you always say," interrupted the Viscount, with the perverse folly of ignorance; "but if I knew as much as you do, it would not make me understand why such ugly creatures need have been made."

"Nor," said the priest, firmly, "is it necessary that you should understand it, particularly if you do not care to inquire. It is enough for you and me if we remember Who made them, some six thousand years before either of us was born."

With which Monsieur the Preceptor (who had all this time kept his place in the little book with his big thumb) returned to the terrace, and resumed his devotions at the point where they had been interrupted which exercise he continued till he was joined by the Cure of the village, and the two priests relaxed in the political and religious gossip of the day.

Monsieur the Viscount rejoined his young guests, and they fed the gold fish and the swans, and played *Colin Maillard* in the shady walks, and made a beautiful bouquet for Madame, and then fled indoors at the first approach of evening chill, and found that the Viscountess had prepared a feast of fruit and flowers for them in the great hall. Here, at the head of the table, with Madame at his right hand, his guests around, and the liveried lacqueys waiting his commands, Monsieur the Viscount forgot that anything had ever been made which could mar beauty and enjoyment; while the two priests outside stalked up and down under the falling twilight, and talked ugly talk of crime and poverty that were *somewhere* now, and of troubles to come hereafter.

And so night fell over the beautiful sky, the beautiful chateau, and the beautiful gardens; and upon the secure slumbers of beautiful Madame and her beautiful son, and beautiful, beautiful France.

*   *   *   *   *

CHAPTER II

It was the year of grace 1792, thirteen years after the events related in the last chapter. It was the 2nd of September, and Sunday, a day of rest and peace in all Christian countries, and even more in gay, beautiful France—a day of festivity and merriment. This Sunday, however, seemed rather an exception to the general rule. There were no gay groups or bannered processions; the typical incense and the public devotion of which it is the symbol were alike wanting; the streets in some places seemed deserted, and in others there was an ominous crowd, and the dreary silence was now and then broken by a distant sound of yells and cries, that struck terror into the hearts of the Parisians.

It was a deserted bye-street, overlooked by some shut-up warehouses, and from the cellar of one of these a young man crept up on to the pathway. His dress had once been beautiful, but it was torn and soiled; his face was beautiful still, but it was marred by the hideous eagerness of a face on which famine has laid her hand—he was starving. As this man came out from the warehouse, another man came down the street. His dress was not beautiful, neither was he. There was a red look about him—he wore a red flannel cap, tricolour ribbons, and had something red upon his hands, which was neither ribbon nor flannel. He also looked hungry; but it was not for food. The other stopped when he saw him, and pulled something from his pocket. It was a watch, a repeater, in a gold filigree case of exquisite workmanship, with raised figures depicting the loves of an Arcadian shepherd and shepherdess; and, as it lay on the white hand of its owner, it bore an evanescent fragrance that seemed to recall scenes as beautiful and as completely past as the days of pastoral perfection, when

"All the world and love were young
And truth in every shepherd's tongue."

The young man held it to the other and spoke. "It was my mother's," he said, with an appealing glance of violet eyes; "I would not part with it but that I am starving. Will you get me food?"

"You are hiding?" said he of the red cap.

"Is that a crime in these days?" said the other, with a smile that would in other days have been irresistible.

The man took the watch, shaded the donor's beautiful face with a rough red cap and tricolour ribbon, and bade him follow him. He, who had but lately come to Paris, dragged his exhausted body after his conductor, hardly noticed the crowds in the streets, the signs by which the man got free passage for them both, or their entrance by a little side-door into a large dark building, and never knew till he was delivered to one of the gaolers that he had been led into the prison of the Abbaye. Then the wretch tore the cap of Liberty from his victim's head, and pointed to him with a fierce laugh.

"He wants food, this aristocrat. He shall not wait long—there is a feast in the court below, which he shall join presently. See to it, Antoine! And you, *Monsieur, Mons-ieur*! listen to the banqueters."

He ceased, and in the silence yells and cries from a court below came up like some horrid answer to imprecation.

The man continued—

"He has paid for his admission, this Monsieur. It belonged to

Madame his mother. Behold!"

He held the watch above his head, and dashed it with insane fury on the ground, and, bidding the gaoler see to his prisoner, rushed away to the court below.

The prisoner needed some attention. Weakness, and fasting, and horror had overpowered a delicate body and a sensitive mind, and he lay senseless by the shattered relic of happier times. Antoine, the gaoler (a weak-minded man whom circumstances had made cruel), looked at him with indifference while the Jacobin remained in the place, and with half-suppressed pity when he had gone. The place where he lay was a hall or passage in the prison, into which several cells opened, and a number of the prisoners were gathered together at one end of it. One of them had watched the proceedings of the Jacobin and his victim with profound interest, and now advanced to where the poor youth lay. He was a priest, and though thirteen years had passed over his head since we saw him in the chateau, and though toil and suffering and anxiety had added the traces of as many more, yet it would not have been difficult to recognize the towering height, the candid face, and, finally, the large thumb in the little book of—, Monsieur the Preceptor, who had years ago exchanged his old position for a parochial cure. He strode up to the gaoler (whose head came a little above the priest's elbow), and, drawing him aside, asked, with his old abruptness, "Who is this?"

"It is the Vicomte de B—. I know his face. He has escaped the commissaires for some days."

"I thought so. Is his name on the registers?"

"No. He escaped arrest, and has just been brought in, as you saw."

Juliana Horatia Ewing

"Antoine," said the priest, in a low voice, and with a gaze that seemed to pierce the soul of the weak little gaoler; "Antoine, when you were a shoemaker in the Rue de la Croix, in two or three hard winters I think you found me a friend."

"Oh! Monsieur le Cure," said Antoine, writhing; "if Monsieur le Cure would believe that if I could save his life! But—"

"Pshaw!" said the priest, "it is not for myself, but for this boy. You must save him, Antoine. Hear me, you *must*. Take him now to one of the lower cells and hide him. You risk nothing. His name is not on the prison register. He will not be called, he will not be missed; that fanatic will think that he has perished with the rest of us (Antoine shuddered, though the priest did not move a muscle) and when this mad fever has subsided and order is restored, he will reward you. And Antoine—"

Here the priest pocketed his book, and somewhat awkwardly with his huge hands unfastened the left side of his cassock, and tore the silk from the lining. Monsieur le Cure's cassock seemed a cabinet of oddities. First he pulled from this ingenious hiding-place a crucifix, which he replaced; then a knot of white ribbon, which he also restored; and, finally, a tiny pocket or bag of what had been cream-coloured satin, embroidered with small bunches of heartsease, and which was aromatic with otto of roses. Awkwardly, and somewhat slowly, he drew out of this a small locket, in the centre of which was some unreadable legend in cabalistic-looking character, and which blazed with the finest diamonds. Heaven alone knows the secret of that gem, or the struggle with which the priest yielded it. He put it into Antoine's hand, talking as he did so partly to himself and partly to the gaoler.

"We brought nothing into this world, and it is certain we can carry nothing out. The diamonds are of the finest, Antoine, and will sell for much. The blessing of a dying priest upon you if you do kindly, and his curse if you do ill to this poor child, whose home was my home in better days. And for the locket—it is but a remembrance, and to remember is not difficult!"

As the last observation was not addressed to Antoine, so also he did not hear it. He was discontentedly watching the body of the Viscount, whom he consented to help, but with genuine weak-mindedness consented ungraciously.

"How am I to get him there? Monsieur le Cure sees that he cannot stand upon his feet."

Monsieur le Cure smiled, and stooping, picked his old pupil up in his arms as if he had been a baby, and bore him to one of the doors.

"You must come no further," said Antoine, hastily.

"Ingrate!" muttered the priest in momentary anger, and then, ashamed, he crossed himself, and pressing the young nobleman to his bosom with the last gush of earthly affection that he was to feel, he kissed his senseless face, spoke a benediction to ears that could not hear it, and laid his burden down.

"GOD the Father, the Son, and the Holy Ghost, be with thee now and in the dread hour of death. Adieu! we shall meet hereafter."

The look of pity, the yearning of rekindled love, the struggle of silenced memories passed from his face and left a shining calm—foretaste of the perpetual Light and the eternal Rest.

Before he reached the other prisoners, the large thumb had found its old place in the little book, the lips formed the old old words; but it might almost have been said of him already, that "his spirit was with the GOD who gave it."

As for Monsieur the Viscount, it was perhaps well that he was not too sensible of his position, for Antoine got him down the flight of stone steps that led to the cell by the simple process of dragging him by the heels. After a similar fashion he crossed the floor, and was deposited on a pallet; the gaoler then emptied a broken pitcher of water over his face, and locking the door securely, hurried back to his charge.

When Monsieur the Viscount came to his senses he raised himself and looked round his new abode. It was a small stone cell; it was underground, with a little grated window at the top that seemed to be level with the court; there was a pallet—painfully pressed and worn—a chair, a stone on which stood a plate and broken pitcher, and in one corner a huge bundle of firewood which mocked a place where there was no fire. Stones lay scattered about, the walls were black, and in the far dark corners the wet oozed out and trickled slowly down, and lizards and other reptiles crawled up.

I suppose that the first object that attracts the hopes of a new prisoner is the window of his cell, and to this, despite his weakness, Monsieur the Viscount crept. It afforded him little satisfaction. It was too high in the cell for him to reach it, too low in the prison to command any view, and was securely grated with iron. Then he examined the walls, but not a stone was loose. As he did so, his eye fell upon the floor, and he noticed that two of the stones that lay about had been raised up by some one and a third laid upon the top. It looked like child's play, and Monsieur the Viscount kicked it down, and then he saw that underneath it there was a pellet of paper roughly rolled together. Evidently it was something left by the former occupant of the cell for his successor. Perhaps he had begun some plan for getting away which he had not had time to perfect on his own account, Perhaps—but by this time the paper was spread out, and Monsieur the Viscount read the writing. The paper was old and yellow. It was the fly-leaf torn out of a little book, and on it was written in black chalk, the words—

"*Souvenez-vous du Sauveur.*" (Remember the Saviour.)

He turned it over, he turned it back again; there was no other mark; there was nothing more; and Monsieur the Viscount did not conceal from himself that he was disappointed. How could it be otherwise? He had been bred in ease and luxury, and surrounded with everything that could make life beautiful; while ugliness, and want, and sickness, and all that make life miserable, had been kept, as far as they can be kept, from the precincts of the beautiful chateau which was his home. What were the *consolations* of religion to him? They are offered to those (and to those only) who need them. They were to Monsieur the Viscount what the Crucified Christ was to the Greeks of old—foolishness.

He put the paper in his pocket and lay down again, feeling it the crowning disappointment of what he had lately suffered. Presently, Antoine came with some food; it was not dainty, but Monsieur the Viscount devoured it like a famished hound, and then made inquiries as to how he came and how long he had been there. When the gaoler began to describe him, whom he called the Cure, Monsieur the Viscount's attention quickened into eagerness, an eagerness deepened by the tender interest that always hangs round the names of those whom we have known in happier and younger days. The happy memories recalled by hearing of his old tutor seemed to blot out his present misfortunes. With French

Juliana Horatia Ewing

excitability, he laughed and wept alternately.

"As burly as ever, you say? The little book? I remember it, it was his breviary. Ah! it is he. It is Monsieur the Preceptor, whom I have not seen for years. Take me to him, bring him here, let me see him!"

But Monsieur the Preceptor was in Paradise.

That first night of Monsieur the Viscount's imprisonment was a terrible one. The bitter chill of a Parisian autumn, the gnawings of half-satisfied hunger, the thick walls that shut out all hope of escape but did not exclude those fearful cries that lasted with few intervals throughout the night, made it like some hideous dream. At last the morning broke; at half-past two o'clock, some members of the *commune* presented themselves in the hall of the National Assembly with the significant announcement:—"The prisons are empty!" and Antoine, who had been quaking for hours, took courage, and went with half a loaf of bread and a pitcher of water to the cell that was not "empty." He found his prisoner struggling with a knot of white ribbon, which he was trying to fasten in his hair. One glance at his face told all.

"It is the fever," said Antoine; and he put down the bread and water and fetched an old blanket and a pillow; and that day and for many days, the gaoler hung above his prisoner's pallet with the tenderness of a woman. Was he haunted by the vision of a burly figure that had bent over his own sick bed in the Rue de la Croix? Did the voice (once so familiar in counsel and benediction!) echo still in his ears?

"The blessing of a dying priest upon you if you do well, and his curse if you do ill to this poor child, whose home was my home in better days."

Be this as it may, Antoine tended his patient with all the constancy compatible with keeping his presence in the prison a secret; and it was not till the crisis was safely past, that he began to visit the cell less frequently, and reassumed the harsh manners which he held to befit his office.

Monsieur the Viscount's mind rambled much in his illness. He called for his mother, who had long been dead. He fancied himself in his own chateau. He thought that all his servants stood in a body before him, but that not one would move to wait on him. He thought that he had abundance of the most tempting food and cooling drinks, but placed just beyond his reach. He thought that he saw two lights like stars near together, which were close to the ground, and kept appearing and then vanishing away. In time he became more sensible; the chateau melted into the stern reality of his prison walls; the delicate food became bread and water; the servants disappeared like spectres; but in the empty cell, in the dark corners near the floor, he still fancied that he saw two sparks of light coming and going, appearing and then vanishing away. He watched them till his giddy head would bear it no longer, and he closed his eyes and slept. When he awoke he was much better, but when he raised himself and turned towards the stone—there, by the bread and the broken pitcher, sat a dirty, ugly, wrinkled toad, gazing at him, Monsieur the Viscount, with eyes of yellow fire.

Monsieur the Viscount had long ago forgotten the toad which had alarmed his childhood; but his national dislike to that animal had not been lessened by years, and the toad of the prison seemed likely to fare no better than the toad of the chateau. He dragged himself from his pallet, and took up one of the large damp stones which lay about the floor of the cell, to throw at the intruder. He expected that when he approached it, the toad would crawl away, and that he could throw the stone after it; but to his surprise, the beast sat quite unmoved, looking at him with calm shining eyes, and, somehow or other, Monsieur the Viscount lacked strength or heart to kill it. He stood doubtful for a moment, and then a sudden feeling of weakness obliged him to drop the stone, and sit down, while tears sprang to his eyes with the sense of his helplessness.

"Why should I kill it?" he said, bitterly. "The beast will live and grow fat upon this damp and loathsomeness, long after they have put an end to my feeble life. It shall remain. The cell is not big, but it is big enough for us both. However large be the rooms a man builds himself to live in, it needs but little space in which to die!"

So Monsieur the Viscount dragged his pallet away from the toad, placed another stone by it, and removed the pitcher; and then, wearied with his efforts, lay down and slept heavily.

When he awoke, on the new stone by the pitcher was the toad, staring full at him with topaz eyes. He lay still this time and did not move, for the animal showed no intention of spitting, and he was puzzled by its tameness.

"It seems to like the sight of a man," he thought. "Is it possible that any former inmate of this wretched prison can have amused his solitude by making a pet of such a creature? and if there were such a man, where is he now?"

Henceforward, sleeping or waking, whenever Monsieur the Viscount lay down upon his pallet, the toad crawled up on to the stone, and kept watch over him with shining lustrous eyes; but whenever there was a sound of the key grating in the lock, and the gaoler coming his rounds, away crept the toad, and was quickly lost in the dark corners of the room. When the man was gone, it returned to its place, and

Monsieur the Viscount would talk to it, as he lay on his pallet.

"Ah! Monsieur Crapaud," he would say, with mournful pleasantry, "without doubt you have had a master and a kind one; but, tell me, who was he, and where is he now? Was he old or young, and was it in the last stage of maddening loneliness that he made friends with such a creature as you?"

Monsieur Crapaud looked very intelligent, but he made no reply, and Monsieur the Viscount had recourse to Antoine.

"Who was in this cell before me?" he asked at the gaoler's next visit.

Antoine's face clouded. "Monsieur le Cure had this room. My orders were that he was to be imprisoned in secret.'"

Monsieur le Cure had this room. There was a revelation in those words. It was all explained now. The priest had always had a love for animals (and for ugly, common animals), which his pupil had by no means shared. His room at the chateau had been little less than a menagerie. He had even kept a glass beehive there, which communicated with a hole in the window through which the bees flew in and out, and he would stand for hours with his thumb in the breviary, watching the labours of his pets. And this also had been his room! This dark, damp cell. Here, breviary in hand, he had stood, and lain, and knelt. Here, in this miserable prison, he had found something to love, and on which to expend the rare intelligence and benevolence of his nature. Here, finally, in the last hours of his life, he had written on the fly-leaf of his prayer-book something to comfort his successor, and, "being dead, yet spoke" the words of consolation which he had administered in his lifetime. Monsieur the Viscount read that paper now with different feelings.

There is, perhaps, no argument so strong, and no virtue that so commands the respect of young men, as consistency. Monsieur the Preceptor's lifelong counsel and example would have done less for his pupil than was effected by the knowledge of his consistent career, now that it was past. It was not the nobility of the priest's principles that awoke in Monsieur the Viscount a desire to imitate his religious example, but the fact that he had applied them to his own life, not only in the time of wealth, but in the time of tribulation and in the hour of death. All that high-strung piety—that life of prayer—those unswerving admonitions to consider the vanity of earthly treasures, and to prepare for death—which had sounded so unreal amidst the perfumed elegances of the chateau, came back now with a reality gained from experiment. The daily life of self-denial, the conversation garnished from Scripture and from the Fathers, had not, after all, been mere priestly affectations. In no symbolic manner, but literally, he had "watched for the coming of his Lord," and "taken up the cross daily;" and so, when the cross was laid on him, and when the voice spoke which must speak to all, "The Master is come, and calleth for thee," he bore the burden and obeyed the summons unmoved.

Unmoved!—this was the fact that struck deep into the heart of Monsieur the Viscount, as he listened to Antoine's account of the Cure's imprisonment. What had astonished and overpowered his own undisciplined nature had not disturbed Monsieur the Preceptor. He had prayed in the chateau—he prayed in the prison. He had often spoken in the chateau of the softening and comforting influences of communion with the lower animals and with nature, and in the uncertainty of imprisonment he had tamed a toad. "None of these things had moved him," and, in a storm of grief and admiration, Monsieur the Viscount bewailed the memory of his tutor.

"If he had only lived to teach me!"

But he was dead, and there was nothing for Monsieur the Viscount but to make the most of his example. This was not so easy to follow as he imagined. Things seemed to be different with him to what they had been with Monsieur the Preceptor. He had no lofty meditations, no ardent prayers, and calm and peace seemed more distant than ever. Monsieur the Viscount met, in short, with all those difficulties that the soul must meet with, which, in a moment of enthusiasm, has resolved upon a higher and a better way of life, and in moments of depression is perpetually tempted to forego that resolution. His prison life was, however, a pretty severe discipline, and he held on with struggles and prayers; and so, little by little, and day by day, as the time of his imprisonment went by, the consolations of religion became a daily strength against the fretfulness of imperious temper, the sickness of hope deferred, and the dark suggestions of despair.

The term of his imprisonment was a long one. Many prisoners came and went within the walls of the Abbaye, but Monsieur the Viscount still remained in his cell; indeed, he would have gained little by leaving it if he could have done so, as he would almost certainly have been retaken. As it was, Antoine on more than one occasion concealed him behind the bundles of firewood, and once or twice he narrowly escaped detection by less friendly officials. There were times when the guillotine seemed to him almost better than this long suspense: but while other heads passed to the block, his remained on his shoulders; and so weeks and even months went by. And during all this time, sleeping or waking, whenever he lay down upon his pallet, the toad crept up on to the stone, and kept watch over him with lustrous eyes.

Monsieur the Viscount hardly acknowledged to himself the affection with which he came to regard this ugly and despicable animal. The greater part of his regard for it he believed to be due to its connection with his tutor, and the rest he set down to the score of his own humanity, and took credit to himself accordingly: whereas in truth Monsieur Crapaud was of incalculable service to his master, who would lie and chatter to him for hours, and almost forget his present discomfort in recalling past happiness, as he described the chateau, the gardens, the burly tutor, and beautiful Madame, or laughed over his childish remembrances of the toad's teeth in Claude Mignon's pocket; whilst Monsieur Crapaud sat well-bred and silent, with a world of comprehension in his fiery eyes. Whoever thinks this puerile must remember that my hero was a Frenchman, and a young Frenchman, with a prescriptive right to chatter for chattering's sake, and also that he had not a very highly cultivated mind of his own to converse with, even if the most highly cultivated intellect is ever a reliable resource against the terrors of solitary confinement.

Foolish or wise, however, Monsieur the Viscount's attachment strengthened daily; and one day something happened which showed his pet in a new light, and afforded him fresh amusement.

The prison was much infested with certain large black spiders, which crawled about the floor and walls; and, as Monsieur the Viscount was lying on his pallet, he saw one of these scramble up and over the stone on which sat Monsieur Crapaud. That good gentleman, whose eyes, till then, had been fixed as usual on his master, now turned his attention to the intruder. The spider, as if conscious of danger, had suddenly stopped still. Monsieur Crapaud gazed at it intently with his beautiful eyes, and bent himself slightly forward. So they remained for some seconds, then the spider turned round, and began suddenly to scramble away. At this instant Monsieur the Viscount saw his friend's eyes gleam with an intenser fire, his head was jerked forwards; it almost seemed as if something had been projected from his mouth, and drawn back again with the rapidity of lightning. Then Monsieur Crapaud resumed his position, drew in his head, and gazed mildly and sedately before him; *but the spider was nowhere to be seen.*

Monsieur the Viscount burst into a loud laugh.

"Eh, well! Monsieur," said he, "but this is not well-bred on your part. Who gave you leave to eat my spiders? and to bolt them in such an unmannerly way, moreover."

In spite of this reproof Monsieur Crapaud looked in no way ashamed of himself, and I regret to state that henceforward (with the partial humaneness of mankind in general), Monsieur the Viscount amused himself by catching the insects (which were only too plentiful) in an old oyster-shell, and then setting them at liberty on the stone for the benefit of his friend. As for him, all appeared to be fish that came to his net—spiders and beetles, slugs and snails from the damp corners, flies, and wood-lice found on turning up the large stone, disappeared one after the other. The wood-lice were an especial amusement: when Monsieur the Viscount touched them, they shut up into tight little balls, and in this condition he removed them to the stone, and placed them like marbles in a row, Monsieur Crapaud watching the proceeding with rapt attention. After awhile the balls would slowly open and begin to crawl away; but he was a very active wood-louse indeed who escaped the suction of Monsieur Crapaud's tongue, as, his eyes glowing with eager enjoyment, he bolted one after another, and Monsieur the Viscount clapped his hands and applauded.

The grated window was a very fine field for spiders and other insects, and by piling up stones on the floor, Monsieur the Viscount contrived to scramble up to it, and fill his friend's oyster-shell with the prey.

One day, about a year and nine months after his first arrival at the prison, he climbed to the embrasure of the window, as usual, oyster-shell in hand. He always chose a time for this when he knew that the court would most probably be deserted, to avoid the danger of being recognized through the grating. He was, therefore, not a little startled at being disturbed in his capture of a fat black spider by a sound of something bumping against the iron bars. On looking up, he saw that a string was dangling before the window with something attached to the end of it. He drew it in, and, as he did so, he fancied that he heard a distant sound of voices and clapped hands, as if from some window above. He proceeded to examine his prize, and found that it was a little round pincushion of sand, such as women use to polish their needles with, and that, apparently, it was used as a make-weight to ensure the steady descent of a neat little letter that was tied beside it, in company with a small lead pencil. The letter was directed to *"The prisoner who finds this."* Monsieur the Viscount opened it at once. This was the letter—

"In prison, 24th Prairial, year 2.

"Fellow-sufferer, who are you? how long have you been imprisoned? Be good enough to answer."

Monsieur the Viscount hesitated for a moment, and then determined to risk all. He tore off a bit of the paper, and with the little pencil hurriedly wrote this reply:—

"In secret, June 12, 1794.

"Louis Archambaud Jean-Marie Arnaud, Vicomte de B., supposed to have perished in the massacres of September, 1792. Keep my secret. I have been imprisoned a year and nine months. Who are you? *how long have* you *been here*?"

The letter was drawn up, and he watched anxiously for the reply. It came, and with it some sheets of blank paper.

"Monsieur,—We have the honour to reply to your inquiries, and thank you for your frankness. Henri Edouard Clermont, Baron de St. Claire. Valerie de St. Claire. We have been here but two days. Accept our sympathy for your misfortunes."

Four words in this note seized at once upon Monsieur the Viscount's interest—*Valerie de St. Claire*;—and for some reasons, which I do not pretend to explain, he decided that it was she who was the author of these epistles, and the demon of curiosity forthwith took possession of his mind. Who was she? was she old or young? And in which relation did she stand to Monsieur le Baron—that of wife, of sister, or of daughter? And from some equally inexplicable cause Monsieur the Viscount determined in his own mind that it was the latter. To make assurance doubly sure, however, he laid a trap to discover the real state of the case. He wrote a letter of thanks and sympathy, expressed with all the delicate chivalrous politeness of a nobleman of the old *regime*, and addressed it to *Madame la Baronne*. The plan succeeded. The next note he received contained these sentences:—"*I am not the Baroness. Madame my mother is, alas! dead. I and my father are alone. He is ill, but thanks you, Monsieur, for your letters, which relieve the* ennui *of imprisonment. Are you alone?*"

Monsieur the Viscount, as in duty bound, relieved the *ennui* of the Baron's captivity by another epistle. Before answering the last question, he turned round involuntarily, and looked to where Monsieur Crapaud sat by the broken pitcher. The beautiful eyes were turned towards him, and Monsieur the Viscount took up his pencil, and wrote hastily, "*I am not alone—I have a friend.*"

Henceforward the oyster-shell took a long time to fill, and patience seemed a harder virtue than ever. Perhaps the last fact had something to do with the rapid decline of Monsieur the Viscount's health. He became paler and weaker, and more fretful. His prayers were accompanied by greater mental struggles, and watered with more tears. He was, however, most positive in his assurances to Monsieur Crapaud that he knew the exact nature and cause of the malady that was consuming him. It resulted, he said, from the noxious and unwholesome condition of his cell; and he would entreat Antoine to have it swept out. After some difficulty the gaoler consented.

It was nearly a month since Monsieur the Viscount had first been startled by the appearance of the little pincushion. The stock of paper had long been exhausted. He had torn up his cambric ruffles to write upon, and Mademoiselle de St. Claire had made havoc of her pocket-handkerchiefs for the same purpose. The Viscount was feebler than ever, and Antoine became alarmed. The cell should be swept out the next morning. He would come himself, he said, and bring another man out of the town with him to help him, for the work was heavy, and he had a touch of rheumatism. The man was a stupid fellow from the country, who had only been a week in Paris; he had never heard of the Viscount, and Antoine would tell him that the prisoner was a certain young lawyer who had really died of fever in prison the day before. Monsieur the Viscount thanked him; and it was not till the next morning arrived, and he was expecting them every moment, that Monsieur the Viscount remembered the toad, and that he would without doubt be swept away with the rest in the general clearance. At first he thought that he would beg them to leave it, but some knowledge of the petty insults which that class of men heaped upon their prisoners made him feel that this would probably be only an additional reason for their taking the animal away. There was no place to hide it in, for they would go all round the room; unless—unless Monsieur the Viscount took it up in his hand. And this was just what he objected to do. All his old feelings of repugnance came back; he had not even got gloves on; his long white hands were bare, he could not touch a toad. It was true that the beast had amused him, and that he had chatted to it; but, after all, this was a piece of childish folly—an unmanly way, to say the least, of relieving the tedium of captivity. What was Monsieur Crapaud but a very ugly (and most people said a venomous) reptile? To what a folly he had been condescending! With these thoughts, Monsieur the Viscount steeled himself against the glances of his topaz-eyed friend, and when the steps of the men were heard upon the stairs, he did not move from the window where he had placed himself, with his back to the stone.

The steps came nearer and nearer, Monsieur the Viscount began to whistle—the key was rattled in the lock, and Monsieur the Viscount heard a bit of bread fall, as the toad hastily descended to hide itself as usual in the corners. In a moment his resolution was gone; another second, and it would be too late. He dashed after the creature, picked it up, and when the men came in he was standing with his hands behind him, in which Monsieur Crapaud was quietly and safely seated.

The room was swept, and Antoine was preparing to go, when the other, who had been eyeing the prisoner suspiciously, stopped and said with a sharp sneer, "Does the citizen always preserve that position?"

"Not he," said the gaoler, good-naturedly. "He spends most of his time in bed, which saves his legs. Come along, Francois."

"I shall not come," said the other, obstinately. "Let the citizen show me his hands."

"Plague take you!" said Antoine, in a whisper. "What sulky fit possesses you, my comrade? Let the poor wretch alone. What wouldst thou with his hands? Wait a little, and thou shall have his head."

"We should have few heads or prisoners either, if thou hadst the care of them," said Francois, sharply. "I say that the prisoner secretes something, and that I will see it. Show your hands, dog of an aristocrat!"

Monsieur the Viscount set his teeth to keep himself from speaking, and held out his hands in silence, toad and all.

Both the men started back with an exclamation, and Francois got behind his comrade, and swore over his shoulder.

Monsieur the Viscount stood upright and still, with a smile on his white face. "Behold, citizen, what I secrete, and what I desire to keep. Behold all that I have left to secrete or to desire! There is nothing more."

"Throw it down!" screamed Francois; "many a witch has been burnt for less—throw it down."

The colour began to flood over Monsieur the Viscount's face; but still he spoke gently, and with bated breath. "If you wish me to suffer, citizen, let this be my witness that I have suffered. I must be very friendless to desire such a friend. I must be brought very low to ask such a favour. Let the

Republic give me this."

"The Republic has one safe rule for aristocrats," said the other; "she gives them nothing but their keep till she pays for their shaving—once for all. She gave one of these dogs a few rags to dress a wound on his back with, and he made a rope of his dressings, and let himself down from the window. We will have no more such games. You may be training the beast to spit poison at good citizens. Throw it down and kill it."

Monsieur the Viscount made no reply. His hands had moved towards his breast, against which he was holding his golden-eyed friend. There are times in life when the brute creation contrasts favourably with the lords thereof, and this was one of them. It was hard to part just now.

Antoine, who had been internally cursing his own folly in bringing such a companion into the cell, now interfered. "If you are going to stay here to be bitten or spit at, Francois, my friend," said he, "I am not. Thou art zealous, my comrade, but dull as an owl. The Republic is far-sighted in her wisdom beyond thy coarse ideas, and has more ways of taking their heads from these aristocrats than one. Dost thou not see?" And he tapped his forehead significantly, and looked at the prisoner; and so, between talking and pushing, got his sulky companion out of the cell, and locked the door after them.

"And so, my friend—my friend!" said Monsieur the Viscount, tenderly, "we are safe once more; but it will not be for long, my Crapaud. Something tells me that I cannot much longer be overlooked. A little while, and I shall be gone; and thou wilt have, perchance, another master, when I am summoned before mine."

Monsieur the Viscount's misgivings were just. Francois, on whose stupidity Antoine had relied, was (as is not uncommon with people stupid in other respects) just clever enough to be mischievous. Antoine's evident alarm made him suspicious, and he began to talk about the too-elegant-looking young lawyer who was imprisoned "in secret," and permitted by the gaoler to keep venomous beasts. Antoine was examined and committed to one of his own cells, and Monsieur the Viscount was summoned before the revolutionary tribunal.

There was little need even for the scanty inquiry that in those days preceded sentence. In every line of his beautiful face, marred as it was by sickness and suffering—in the unconquerable dignity, which dirt and raggedness were powerless to hide, the fatal nobility of his birth and breeding were betrayed. When he returned to the ante-room, he did not positively know his fate; but in his mind there was a moral certainty that left him no hope.

The room was filled with other prisoners awaiting trial; and, as he entered, his eyes wandered round it to see if there were any familiar faces. They fell upon two figures standing with their backs to him—a tall, fierce-looking man, who, despite his height and fierceness, had a restless, nervous despondency expressed in all his movements; and a young girl who leant on his arm as if for support, but whose steady quietude gave her more the air of a supporter. Without seeing their faces, and for no reasonable reason, Monsieur the Viscount decided with himself that they were the Baron and his daughter, and he begged the man who was conducting him for a moment's delay. The man consented. France was becoming sick of unmitigated carnage, and even the executioners sometimes indulged in pity by way of a change.

As Monsieur the Viscount approached the two they turned round, and he saw her face—a very fair and very resolute one, with ashen hair and large eyes. In common with almost all the faces in that room, it was blanched with suffering; and, it is fair to say, in common with many of them, it was pervaded by a lofty calm. Monsieur the Viscount never for an instant doubted his own conviction; he drew near and said in a low voice, "Mademoiselle de St. Claire!"

The Baron looked first fierce, and then alarmed. His daughter's face illumined; she turned her large eyes on the speaker, and said simply, "Monsieur le Vicomte?"

The Baron apologized, commiserated, and sat down on a seat near, with a look of fretful despair; and his daughter and Monsieur the Viscount were left standing together. Monsieur the Viscount desired to say a great deal, and could say very little. The moments went by, and hardly a word had been spoken.

Valerie asked if he knew his fate.

"I have not heard it," he said; "but I am morally certain. There can be but one end in these days."

She sighed. "It is the same with us. And if you must suffer, Monsieur, I wish that we may suffer together. It would comfort my father—and me."

Her composure vexed him. Just, too, when he was sensible that the desire of life was making a few fierce struggles in his own breast.

"You seem to look forward to death with great cheerfulness, Mademoiselle."

The large eyes were raised to him with a look of surprise at the irritation of his tone.

"I think," she said, gently, "that one does not look forward *to*, but *beyond* it." She stopped and hesitated, still watching his face, and then spoke hurriedly and diffidently:—

"Monsieur, it seems impertinent to make such suggestions to you, who have doubtless a full fund of consolation; but I remember, when a child, going to hear the preaching of a monk who was famous for his eloquence. He said that his text was from the Scriptures—it has been in my mind all to-day—'*There the wicked cease from troubling, and there the weary be at rest.*' The man is becoming impatient. Adieu! Monsieur. A thousand thanks and a thousand blessings."

She offered her cheek, on which there was not a ray of increased colour, and Monsieur the Viscount stooped and kissed it, with a thick mist gathering in his eyes, through which he could not see her face.

"Adieu! Valerie!"

"Adieu! Louis!"

So they met, and so they parted; and as Monsieur the Viscount went back to his prison, he flattered himself that the last link was broken for him in the chain of earthly interests.

When he reached the cell he was tired, and lay down, and in a few seconds a soft scrambling over the floor announced the return of Monsieur Crapaud from his hiding-place. With one wrinkled leg after another he clambered on to the stone, and Monsieur the Viscount started when he saw him.

"Friend Crapaud! I had actually forgotten thee. I fancied I had said adieu for the last time;" and he gave a choked sigh, which Monsieur Crapaud could not be expected to understand. In about five minutes he sprang up suddenly. "Monsieur Crapaud, I have not long to live, and no time must be lost in making my will." Monsieur Crapaud was too wise to express any astonishment; and his master began to hunt for a tidy-looking stone (paper and cambric were both at an end). They were all rough and dirty; but necessity had made the Viscount inventive, and he took a couple and rubbed them together till he had polished both. Then he pulled out the little pencil, and for the next half hour composed and wrote busily. When it was done he lay down, and read it to his friend. This was Monsieur the Viscount's last will and Testament:—

"*To my successor in this cell.*

"To you whom Providence has chosen to be the inheritor of my sorrows and my captivity, I desire to make another bequest. There is in this prison a toad. He was tamed by a man (peace to his memory!) who tenanted this cell before me. He has been my friend and companion for nearly two years of sad imprisonment. He has sat by my bedside, fed from my hand, and shared all my confidence. He is ugly, but he has beautiful eyes; he is silent, but he is attentive; he is a brute, but I wish the men of France were in this respect more his superiors! He is very faithful. May you never have a worse friend! He feeds upon insects, which I have been accustomed to procure for him. Be kind to him; he will repay it. Like other men, I bequeath what I would take with me if I could.

"Fellow-sufferer, adieu! GOD comfort you as He has comforted me! The sorrows of this life are sharp but short; the joys of the next life are eternal. Think sometimes on him who commends his friend to your pity, and himself to your prayers.

"This is the last will and testament of Louis Archambaud

Jean-Marie Arnaud, Vicomte de B—."

Monsieur the Viscount's last will and testament was with difficulty squeezed into the surface of the larger of the stones. Then he hid it where the priest had hidden *his* bequest long ago, and then lay down to dream of Monsieur the Preceptor, and that they had met at last.

The next day was one of anxious suspense. In the evening, as usual, a list of those who were to be guillotined next morning, was brought into the prison; and Monsieur the Viscount begged for a sight of it. It was brought to him. First on the list was Antoine! Halfway down was his own name, "Louis de B—," and a little lower his fascinated gaze fell upon names that stirred his heart with such a passion of regret as he had fancied it would never feel again, "Henri de St. Claire, Valerie de St. Claire."

Her eyes seemed to shine on him from the gathering twilight, and her calm voice to echo in his ears. "*It has been in my mind all to-day. There the wicked cease from troubling, and there the weary be at rest.*"

There! He buried his face and prayed.

He was disturbed by the unlocking of the door, and the new gaoler appeared with Antoine! The poor wretch seemed overpowered by terror. He had begged to be imprisoned for this last night with Monsieur the Viscount. It was only a matter of a few hours, as they were to die at daybreak, and his request was granted.

Antoine's entrance turned the current of Monsieur the Viscount's thoughts. No more selfish reflections now. He must comfort this poor creature, of whose death he was to be the unintentional cause. Antoine's first anxiety was that

Monsieur the Viscount should bear witness that the gaoler had treated him kindly, and so earned the blessing and not the curse of Monsieur le Cure, whose powerful presence seemed to haunt him still. On this score he was soon set at rest, and then came the old, old story. He had been but a bad man. If his life were to come over again, he would do differently. Did Monsieur the Viscount think that there was any hope?

Would Monsieur the Viscount have recognized himself, could he, two years ago, have seen himself as he was now? Kneeling by that rough, uncultivated figure, and pleading with all the eloquence that he could master to that rough uncultivated heart, the great Truths of Christianity—so great and few and simple in their application to our needs! The violet eyes had never appealed more tenderly, the soft voice had never been softer than now, as he strove to explain to this ignorant soul, the cardinal doctrines of Faith and Repentance, and Charity, with an earnestness that was perhaps more effectual than his preaching.

Monsieur the Viscount was quite as much astonished as flattered by the success of his instructions. The faith on which he had laid hold with such mortal struggles, seemed almost to "come natural" (as people say) to Antoine. With abundant tears he professed the deepest penitence for his past life, at the same time that he accepted the doctrine of the Atonement as a natural remedy, and never seemed to have a doubt in the Infinite Mercy that should cover his infinite guilt.

It was all so orthodox that even if he had doubted (which he did not) the sincerity of the gaoler's contrition and belief, Monsieur the Viscount could have done nothing but envy the easy nature of Antoine's convictions. He forgot the difference of their respective capabilities!

When the night was far advanced the men rose from their knees, and Monsieur the Viscount persuaded Antoine to lie down on his pallet, and when the gaoler's heavy breathing told that he was asleep, Monsieur the Viscount felt relieved to be alone once more—alone, except for Monsieur Crapaud, whose round fiery eyes were open as usual.

The simplicity with which he had been obliged to explain the truths of Divine Love to Antoine, was of signal service to Monsieur the Viscount himself. It left him no excuse for those intricacies of doubt, with which refined minds too often torture themselves; and as he paced feebly up and down the cell, all the long-withheld peace for which he had striven since his imprisonment seemed to flood into his soul. How blessed—how undeservedly blessed—was his fate! Who or what was he that after such short, such mitigated sufferings, the crown of victory should be so near? The way had seemed long to come, it was short to look back upon, and now the golden gates were almost reached, the everlasting doors were open. A few more hours, and then—! and as Monsieur the Viscount buried his worn face in his hands, the tears that trickled from his fingers were literally tears of joy.

He groped his way to the stone, pushed some straw close to it, and lay down on the ground to rest, watched by Monsieur's Crapaud's fiery eyes. And as he lay, faces seemed to him to rise out of the darkness, to take the form and features of the face of the priest, and to gaze at him with unutterable benediction. And in his mind, like some familiar piece of music, awoke the words that had been written on the fly-leaf of the little book; coming back, sleepily and dreamily, over and over again—

"*Souvenez-vous du Sauveur! Souvenez-vous du Sauveur!*"

(Remember the Saviour!)

In that remembrance he fell asleep.

Monsieur the Viscount's sleep for some hours was without a dream. Then it began to be disturbed by that uneasy consciousness of sleeping too long, which enables some people to awake at whatever hour they have resolved upon. At last it became intolerable, and wearied as he was, he awoke. It was broad daylight, and Antoine was snoring beside him. Surely the cart would come soon, the executions were generally at an early hour. But time went on, and no one came, and Antoine awoke. The hours of suspense passed heavily, but at last there were steps and a key rattled into the lock. The door opened, and the gaoler appeared with a jug of milk and a loaf. With a strange smile he set them down.

"A good appetite to you, citizens."

Antoine flew on him. "Comrade! we used to be friends. Tell me, what is it? Is the execution deferred?"

"The execution has taken place at last," said the other, significantly; "*Robespierre is dead!*" and he vanished.

Antoine uttered a shriek of joy. He wept, he laughed, he cut capers, and flinging himself at Monsieur the Viscount's feet, he kissed them rapturously. When he raised his eyes to Monsieur the Viscount's face, his transports moderated. The last shock had been too much, he seemed almost in a stupor. Antoine got him on to the pallet, dragged the blanket over him, broke the bread into the milk, and played the nurse once more.

On that day thousands of prisoners in the city of Paris alone awoke from the shadow of death to the hope of life. The Reign of Terror was ended!

Juliana Horatia Ewing

CHAPTER III

It was a year of Grace early in the present century.

We are again in the beautiful country of beautiful France. It is the chateau once more. It is the same, but changed. The unapproachable elegance, the inviolable security, have witnessed invasion. The right wing of the chateau is in ruins, with traces of fire upon the blackened walls; while here and there, a broken statue or a roofless temple are sad memorials of the Revolution. Within the restored part of the chateau, however, all looks well. Monsieur the Viscount has been fortunate, and if not so rich a man as his father, has yet regained enough of his property to live with comfort, and, as he thinks, luxury. The long rooms are little less elegant than in former days, and Madame the present Viscountess's boudoir is a model of taste. Not far from it is another room, to which it forms a singular contrast. This room belongs to Monsieur the Viscount. It is small, with one window. The floor and walls are bare, and it contains no furniture; but on the floor is a worn-out pallet, by which lies a stone, and on that a broken pitcher, and in a little frame against the wall is preserved a crumpled bit of paper like the fly-leaf of some little book, on which is a half-effaced inscription, which can be deciphered by Monsieur the Viscount if by no one else. Above the window is written in large letters, a date and the word REMEMBER. Monsieur the Viscount is not likely to forget, but he is afraid of himself and of prosperity lest it should spoil him.

It is evening, and Monsieur the Viscount is strolling along the terrace with Madame on his arm. He has only one to offer her, for where the other should be an empty sleeve is pinned to his breast, on which a bit of ribbon is stirred by the breeze. Monsieur the Viscount has not been idle since we saw him last; the faith that taught him to die, has taught him also how to live—an honourable, useful life.

It is evening, and the air comes up perfumed from a bed of violets by which Monsieur the Viscount is kneeling. Madame (who has a fair face and ashen hair) stands by him with her little hand on his shoulder, and her large eyes upon the violets.

"My friend! my friend! my friend!" It is Monsieur the Viscount's voice, and at the sound of it, there is a rustle among the violets that sends the perfume high into the air. Then from the parted leaves come forth first a dirty wrinkled leg, then a dirty wrinkled head with gleaming eyes, and Monsieur Crapaud crawls with self-satisfied dignity on to Monsieur the Viscount's outstretched hand.

So they stay laughing and chatting, and then Monsieur the Viscount bids his friend good-night, and holds him towards Madame that she may do the same. But Madame (who did not enjoy Monsieur Crapaud's society in prison) cannot be induced to do more than scratch his head delicately with the tip of her white finger. But she respects him greatly, at a distance, she says. Then they go back along the terrace, and are met by a man-servant in Monsieur the Viscount's livery. Is it possible that this is Antoine, with his shock head covered with powder?

Yes; that grating voice, which no mental change avails to subdue, is his, and he announces that Monsieur le Cure has arrived. It is the old Cure of the village (who has survived the troubles of the Revolution), and many are the evenings he spends at the chateau, and many the times in which the closing acts of a noble life are recounted to him, the life of his old friend whom he hopes ere long to see—of Monsieur the Preceptor. He is kindly welcomed by Monsieur and by

Madame, and they pass on together into the chateau. And when Monsieur the Viscount's steps have ceased to echo from the terrace, Monsieur Crapaud buries himself once more among the violets.

* * * * *

Monsieur the Viscount is dead, and Madame sleeps also at his side; and their possessions have descended to their son.

Not the least valued among them is a case with a glass front and sides, in which, seated upon a stone is the body of a toad stuffed with exquisite skill, from whose head gleam eyes of genuine topaz. Above it in letters of gold is a date, and this inscription:—

"MONSIEUR THE VISCOUNT'S FRIEND."

ADIEU!

THE YEW-LANE GHOSTS

CHAPTER I

"Cowards are cruel."

—OLD PROVERB

This story begins on a fine autumn afternoon when, at the end of a field over which the shadows of a few wayside trees were stalking like long thin giants, a man and a boy sat side by side upon a stile. They were not a happy-looking pair. The boy looked uncomfortable, because he wanted to get away and dared not go. The man looked uncomfortable also; but then no one had ever seen him look otherwise, which was the more strange as he never professed to have any object in life but his own pleasure and gratification. Not troubling himself with any consideration of law or principle—of his own duty or other people's comfort—he had consistently spent his whole time and energies in trying to be jolly; and though now a grown-up young man, had so far had every appearance of failing in the attempt. From this it will be seen that he was not the most estimable of characters, and we shall have no more to do with him than we can help; but as he must appear in the story, he may as well be described.

If constant self-indulgence had answered as well as it should have done, he would have been a fine-looking young man; as it was, the habits of his life were fast destroying his appearance. His hair would have been golden if it had been kept clean. His figure was tall and strong; but the custom of slinking about places where he had no business to be, and lounging in corners where he had nothing to do, had given it such a hopeless slouch that for the matter of beauty he might almost as well have been knock-kneed. His eyes would have been handsome if the lids had been less red; and if he had ever looked you in the face, you would have seen that they were blue. His complexion was fair by nature and discoloured by drink. His manner was something between a sneak and a swagger, and he generally wore his cap a-one-side, carried his hands in his pockets and a short stick under his arm, and whistled when any one passed him. His chief characteristic, perhaps, was the habit he had of kicking. Indoors he kicked the furniture, in the road he kicked the stones, if he lounged against a wall he kicked it; he kicked all animals and such human beings as he felt sure would not kick him again.

It should be said here that he had once announced his intention of "turning steady, and settling, and getting wed." The object of his choice was the prettiest girl in the village, and was as good as she was pretty. To say the truth, the time had been when Bessy had not felt unkindly towards the yellow-haired lad; but his conduct had long put a gulf between them, which only the conceit of a scamp would have attempted to pass. However, he flattered himself that he "knew what the lasses meant when they said no;" and on the strength of this knowledge he presumed far enough to elicit a rebuff so hearty and unmistakable that for a week he was the laughing stock of the village. There was no mistake this time as to what "no" meant; his admiration turned to a hatred almost as intense, and he went faster "to the bad" than ever.

It was Bessy's little brother who sat by him on the stile; "Beauty Bill," as he was called, from the large share he possessed of the family good looks. The lad was one of those people who seem born to be favourites. He was handsome, and merry, and intelligent; and, being well brought up, was well-conducted and amiable—the pride and pet of the village. Why did Mother Muggins of the shop let the goody side of her scales of justice drop the lower by one lollipop for Bill than for any other lad, and exempt him by unwonted smiles from her general anathema on the urchin race? There were other honest boys in the parish, who paid for their treacle-sticks in sterling copper of the realm! The very roughs of the village were proud of him, and would have showed their good nature in ways little to his benefit had not his father kept a somewhat severe watch upon his habits and conduct. Indeed, good parents and a strict home counterbalanced the evils of popularity with Beauty Bill, and, on the whole, he was little spoilt, and well deserved the favour he met with. It was under cover of friendly patronage that his companion was now detaining him; but, all the circumstances considered, Bill felt more suspicious than gratified, and wished Bully Tom anywhere but where he was.

The man threw out one leg before him like the pendulum of a clock.

"Night school's opened, eh?" he inquired; and back swung the pendulum against Bill's shins.

"Yes;" and the boy screwed his legs on one side.

"You don't go, do you?"

"Yes, I do," said Bill, trying not to feel ashamed of the fact, "Father can't spare me to the day-school now, so our Bessy persuaded him to let me go at nights."

Bully Tom's face looked a shade darker, and the pendulum took a swing which it was fortunate the lad avoided; but the conversation continued with every appearance of civility.

"You come back by Yew-lane, I suppose?"

"Yes."

"Why, there's no one lives your way but old Johnson; you must come back alone?"

"Of course, I do," said Bill, beginning to feel vaguely uncomfortable.

"It must be dark now before school looses?" was the next inquiry; and the boy's discomfort increased, he hardly knew why, as he answered—

"There's a moon."

"So there is," said Bully Tom, in a tone of polite assent; "and there's a weathercock on the church-steeple but I never heard of either of 'em coming down to help a body, whatever happened."

Bill's discomfort had become alarm.

"Why, what could happen?" he asked. "I don't understand you."

His companion whistled, looked up in the air, and kicked vigorously, but said nothing. Bill was not extraordinarily brave, but he had a fair amount both of spirit and sense; and having a shrewd suspicion that Bully Tom was trying to frighten him, he almost made up his mind to run off then and there. Curiosity, however, and a vague alarm which he could not throw off, made him stay for a little more information.

"I wish you'd out with it!" he exclaimed, impatiently. "What could happen? No one ever comes along Yew-lane; and if they did they wouldn't hurt me."

"I know no one ever comes near it when they can help it," was the reply; "so, to be sure, you couldn't get set upon. And a pious lad of your sort wouldn't mind no other kind. Not like ghosts, or anything of that."

And Bully Tom looked round at his companion; a fact disagreeable from its rarity.

"I don't believe in ghosts," said Bill, stoutly.

"Of course you don't," sneered his tormentor; "you're too well educated. Some people does, though. I suppose them that has seen them does. Some people thinks that murdered men walk. P'raps some people thinks the man as was murdered in Yew-lane walks."

"What man?" gasped Bill, feeling very chilly down the spine.

"Him that was riding by the cross-roads and dragged into Yew-lane, and his head cut off and never found, and his body buried in the churchyard," said Bully Tom, with a rush of superior information; "and all I know is, if I thought he walked in Yew-lane, or any other lane, I wouldn't go within five mile of it after dusk—that's all. But then I'm not book-larned."

The two last statements were true if nothing else was that the man had said; and after holding up his feet and examining his boots with his head a-one-side, as if considering their probable efficiency against flesh and blood, he slid from his perch, and "loafed" slowly up the street, whistling and kicking the stones as he went along. As to Beauty Bill, he fled home as fast as his legs would carry him. By the door stood Bessy, washing some clothes; who turned her pretty face as he came up.

"You're late, Bill," she said. "Go in and get your tea, it's set out. It's night-school night, thou knows, and Master Arthur always likes his class to time." He lingered, and she continued—"John Gardener was down this afternoon about some potatoes, and he says Master Arthur is expecting a friend."

Bill did not heed this piece of news, any more than the slight flush on his sister's face as she delivered it; he was wondering whether what Bully Tom said was mere invention to frighten him, or whether there was any truth in it.

"Bessy!" he said, "was there a man ever murdered in Yew-lane?"

Bessy was occupied with her own thoughts, and did not notice the anxiety of the question.

"I believe there was," she answered carelessly, "somewhere about there. It's a hundred years ago or more. There's an old gravestone over him in the churchyard by the wall, with an odd verse on it. They say the parish clerk wrote it. But get your tea, or you'll be late, and father'll be angry;" and Bessy took up her tub and departed.

Poor Bill! Then it was too true. He began to pull up his trousers and look at his grazed legs; and the thoughts of his aching shins, Bully Tom's cruelty, the unavoidable night-school, and the possible ghost, were too much for him, and he burst into tears.

CHAPTER II

"There are birds out on the bushes,
In the meadows lies the lamb,
How I wonder if they're ever
Half as frightened as I am?"

—C.F. ALEXANDER

The night-school was drawing to a close. The attendance had been good, and the room looked cheerful. In one corner the Rector was teaching a group of grown-up men, who (better late than never) were zealously learning to read; in another the schoolmaster was flourishing his stick before a map as he concluded his lesson in geography. By the fire sat Master Arthur, the Rector's son, surrounded by his class, and in front of him stood Beauty Bill. Master Arthur was very popular with the people, especially with his pupils. The boys were anxious to get into his class, and loath to leave it. They admired his great height, his merry laugh, the variety of walking-sticks he brought with him, and his very funny way of explaining pictures. He was not a very methodical teacher, and was rather apt to give unexpected lessons on subjects in which he happened just then to be interested himself; but he had a clear simple way of explaining anything, which impressed it on the memory, and he took a great deal of pains in his own way. Bill was especially devoted to him. He often wished that Master Arthur could get very rich, and take him for his man-servant; he thought he should like to brush his clothes and take care of his sticks. He had a great interest in the growth of his moustache and whiskers. For some time past Master Arthur had had a trick of pulling at his upper lip whilst he was teaching; which occasionally provoked a whisper of "Moostarch, guvernor!" between two unruly members of his class; but never till to-night had Bill seen

Juliana Horatia Ewing

anything in that line which answered his expectations. Now, however, as he stood before the young gentleman, the fire-light fell on such a distinct growth of hair, that Bill's interest became absorbed to the exclusion of all but the most perfunctory attention to the lesson on hand. Would Master Arthur grow a beard? Would his moustache be short like the pictures of Prince Albert, or long and pointed like that of some other great man whose portrait he had seen in the papers? He was calculating on the probable effect of either style, when the order was given to put away books, and then the thought which had been for a time diverted came back again—his walk home.

Poor Bill! his fears returned with double force from having been for awhile forgotten. He dawdled over the books, he hunted in wrong places for his cap and comforter, he lingered till the last boy had clattered through the doorway, and left him with a group of elders who closed the proceedings and locked up the school. But after this further delay was impossible. The whole party moved out into the moonlight, and the Rector and his son, the schoolmaster and the teachers, commenced, a sedate parish gossip, whilst Bill trotted behind, wondering whether any possible or impossible business would take one of them his way. But when the turning point was reached, the Rector destroyed all his hopes.

"None of us go your way, I think," said he, as lightly as if there were no grievance in the case; "however, it's not far. Good-night, my boy!"

And so with a volley of good-nights, the cheerful voices passed on up the village. Bill stood till they had quite died away, and then when all was silent, he turned into the lane.

The cold night-wind crept into his ears, and made

uncomfortable noises among the trees, and blew clouds over the face of the moon. He almost wished that there were no moon. The shifting shadows under his feet, and the sudden patches of light on unexpected objects, startled him, and he thought he should have felt less frightened if it had been quite dark. Once he ran for a bit, then he resolved to be brave, then to be reasonable; he repeated scraps of lessons, hymns, and last Sunday's Collect, to divert and compose his mind; and as this plan seemed to answer, he determined to go through the Catechism, both question and answer, which he hoped might carry him to the end of his unpleasant journey. He had just asked himself a question with considerable dignity, and was about to reply, when a sudden gleam of moonlight lit up a round object in the ditch. Bill's heart seemed to grow cold, and he thought his senses would have forsaken him. Could this be the head of—? No! on nearer inspection it proved to be only a turnip; and when one came to think of it, that would have been rather a conspicuous place for the murdered man's skull to have been lost in for so many years.

My hero must not be ridiculed too much for his fears. The terrors that visit childhood are not the less real and over-powering from being unreasonable; and to excite them is wanton cruelty. Moreover, he was but a little lad, and had been up and down Yew-lane both in daylight and dark without any fears, till Bully Tom's tormenting suggestions had alarmed him. Even now, as he reached the avenue of yews from which the lane took its name, and passed into their gloomy shade, he tried to be brave. He tried to think of the good GOD Who takes care of His children, and to Whom the darkness and the light are both alike. He thought of all he had been taught about angels, and wondered if one were near him now, and wished that he could see him, as Abraham and other good people had seen angels. In short, the poor lad did his best to apply what he had been taught to the present emergency, and very likely had he not done so he would have been worse; but as it was, he was not a little frightened, as we shall see.

Yew-lane—cool and dark when the hottest sunshine lay beyond it—a loitering place for lovers—the dearly-loved play-place of generations of children on sultry summer days—looked very grim and vault-like, with narrow streaks of moonlight peeping in at rare intervals to make the darkness to be felt! Moreover, it was really damp and cold, which is not favourable to courage. At a certain point Yew-lane skirted a corner of the churchyard, and was itself crossed by another road, thus forming a "four-want-way," where suicides were buried in times past. This road was the old high-road, where the mail coach ran, and along which, on such a night as this, a hundred years ago, a horseman rode his last ride. As he passed the church on his fatal journey did anything warn him how soon his headless body would be buried beneath its shadow? Bill wondered. He wondered if he were old or young—what sort of a horse he rode—whose cruel hands dragged him into the shadow of the yews and slew him, and where his head was hidden, and why. Did the church look just the same, and the moon shine just as brightly, that night a century ago? Bully Tom was right. The weathercock and moon sit still, whatever happens. The boy watched the gleaming high road as it lay beyond the dark aisle of trees, till he fancied he could hear the footfalls of the solitary horse—and yet, no! The sound was not upon the hard road, but nearer; it was not the clatter of hoofs, but something—and a rustle—and then Bill's blood seemed to freeze in his veins, as he saw a white figure, wrapped in what seemed to be a shroud, glide out of the shadow of the yews and move slowly down the lane. When it reached the road it paused, raised a long arm warningly towards him for a moment, and then vanished in the direction of the churchyard.

What would have been the consequence of the intense fright the poor lad experienced is more than anyone can say, if at that moment the church clock had not begun to strike nine. The familiar sound, close in his ears, roused him from the first shock, and before it had ceased he contrived to make a desperate rally of his courage, flew over the road, and crossed the two fields that now lay between him and home without looking behind him.

CHAPTER III

"It was to her a real *grief of heart*, acute, as children's sorrows often are.

"We beheld this from the opposite windows—and, seen thus from a little distance, how many of our own and of other people's sorrows might not seem equally trivial, and equally deserving of ridicule!"

—HANS CHRISTIAN ANDERSEN

When Bill got home he found the household busy with a much more practical subject than that of ghosts and haunted yew-trees. Bessy was ill. She had felt a pain in her side all the day, which towards night had become so violent that the doctor was sent for, who had pronounced it pleurisy, and had sent her to bed. He was just coming downstairs as Bill burst into the house. The mother was too much occupied about her daughter to notice the lad's condition; but the doctor's sharp eyes saw that something was amiss, and he at once inquired what it was. Bill hammered and stammered, and stopped short. The doctor was such a tall, stout, comfortable-looking man, he looked as if he couldn't believe in ghosts. A slight frown, however, had come over his comfortable face, and he laid two fingers on Bill's wrist as he repeated his question. "Please, sir," said Bill, "I've seen—"

"A mad dog?" suggested the doctor.

"No, sir."

"A mad bull?"

"No, sir," said Bill, desperately, "I've seen a ghost."

The doctor exploded into a fit of laughter, and looked more comfortable than ever.

"And *where* did we see the ghost?" he inquired, in a professional voice, as he took up his coat-tails and warmed himself at the fire.

"In Yew-lane, sir; and I'm sure I did see it," said Bill, half crying; "it was all in white, and beckoned me."

"That's to say you saw a white gravestone, or a tree in the moonlight, or one of your classmates dressed up in a table-cloth. It was all moonshine, depend upon it," said the doctor, with a chuckle at his own joke; "take my advice, my boy, and don't give way to foolish fancies."

At this point the mother spoke—

"If his father knew, sir, as he'd got any such fads in his head, he'd soon flog 'em out of him."

"His father is a very good one," said the doctor; "a little too fond of the stick, perhaps. There," he added, good-naturedly, slipping sixpence into Bill's hand, "get a new knife, my boy, and cut a good thick stick, and the next ghost you meet, lay hold of him and let him taste it."

Bill tried to thank him, but somehow his voice was choked, and the doctor turned to his mother.

"The boy has been frightened," he said, "and is upset. Give him some supper, and put him to bed." And the good gentleman departed.

Bill was duly feasted and sent to rest. His mother did not mention the matter to her husband, as she knew he would be angry; and occupied with real anxiety for her daughter, she soon forgot it herself. Consequently, the next night-school night she sent Bill to "clean himself," hurried on his tea, and packed him off, just as if nothing had happened.

The boy's feelings since the night of the apparition had not been enviable. He could neither eat nor sleep. As he lay in bed at night, he kept his face covered with the clothes, dreading that if he peeped out into the room the phantom of the murdered horseman would beckon to him from the dark corners. Lying so till the dawn broke and the cocks began to crow, he would then look cautiously forth, and seeing by the grey light that the corners were empty, and that the figure by the door was not the Yew-lane Ghost, but his mother's faded print dress hanging on a nail, would drop his head and fall wearily asleep. The day was no better, for each hour brought him nearer to the next night school; and Bessy's illness made his mother so busy, that he never could find the right moment to ask her sympathy for his fears, and still less could he feel himself able to overcome them. And so the night-school came round again, and there he sat, gulping down a few mouthfuls of food, and wondering how he should begin to tell his mother that he neither dare, could, nor would, go down Yew-lane again at night. He had just opened his lips when the father came in, and asked in a loud voice "Why Bill was not off." This effectually put a stop to any confidences, and the boy ran out of the house. Not, however, to school. He made one or two desperate efforts at determination, and then gave up altogether. He *could* not go!

He was wondering what he should do with himself, when it struck him that he would go whilst it was daylight and look for the grave with the odd verse of which Bessy had spoken. He had no difficulty in finding it. It was marked by a large ugly stone, on which the inscription was green and in some places almost effaced.

SACRED TO THE MEMORY

OF

EPHRAIM GARNETT—

He had read so far when a voice close by him said—

"You'll be late for school, young chap."

Bill looked up, and to his horror beheld Bully Tom standing in the road and kicking the churchyard wall.

"Aren't you going?" he asked, as Bill did not speak.

"Not to-night," said Bill, with crimson cheeks.

"Larking, eh?" said Bully Tom. "My eyes, won't your father give it you!" and he began to move off.

"Stop!" shouted Bill in an agony; "don't tell him, Tom. That would be a dirty trick. I'll go next time, I will indeed; I can't go to-night. I'm not larking, I'm scared. You won't tell?"

"Not this time, maybe," was the reply; "but I wouldn't be in your shoes if you play this game next night;" and off he went.

Bill thought it well to quit the churchyard at once for some place where he was not likely to be seen; he had never played truant before, and for the next hour or two was thoroughly miserable as he slunk about the premises of a neighbouring farm, and finally took refuge in a shed, and began to consider his position. He would remain hidden till nine o'clock, and then go home. If nothing were said, well and good; unless some accident should afterwards betray him. But if his mother asked any questions about the school? He dared not, and he would not, tell a lie; and yet what would be the result of the truth coming out? There could be no doubt that his father would beat him. Bill thought again, and decided that he could bear a thrashing, but not the sight of the Yew-lane Ghost; so he remained where he was, wondering how it would be, and how he should get over the next school-night when it came. The prospect was so hopeless, and the poor lad so wearied with anxiety and wakeful nights, that he was almost asleep when he was startled by the church clock striking nine; and, jumping up, he ran home. His heart beat heavily as he crossed the threshold; but his mother was still absorbed by thoughts of Bessy, and he went to bed unquestioned. The next day too passed over without any awkward remarks, which was very satisfactory; but then night-school day came again, and Bill felt that he was in a worse position than ever. He had played truant once with success; but he was aware that it would not do a second time. Bully Tom was spiteful, and Master Arthur might come to "look up" his recreant pupil, and then Bill's father would know all.

On the morning of the much-dreaded day, his mother sent him up to the Rectory to fetch some little delicacy that had been promised for Bessy's dinner. He generally found it rather amusing to go there. He liked to peep at the pretty garden, to look out for Master Arthur, and to sit in the kitchen and watch the cook, and wonder what she did with all the dishes and bright things that decorated the walls. To-day all was quite different. He avoided the gardens, he was afraid of being seen by his teacher, and though cook had an unusual display of pots and pans in operation, he sat in the corner of the kitchen indifferent to everything but the thought of the Yew-lane Ghost. The dinner for Bessy was put between two saucers, and as cook gave it into his hands she asked kindly after his sister, and added—

"You don't look over-well yourself, lad! What's amiss?"

Bill answered that he was quite well, and hurried out of the house to avoid further inquiries. He was becoming afraid of everyone! As he passed the garden he thought of the gardener, and wondered if he would help him. He was very young and very good-natured; he had taken of late to coming to see Bessy, and Bill had his own ideas upon that point; finally, he had a small class at the night-school. Bill wondered whether if he screwed up his courage to-night to go, John Gardener would walk back with him for the pleasure of hearing the latest accounts of Bessy. But all hopes of this sort were cut off by Master Arthur's voice shouting to him from the garden—

"Hi, there! I want you, Willie! Come here, I say."

Bill ran through the evergreens, and there among the flower-beds in the sunshine he saw—first, John Gardener driving a mowing-machine over the velvety grass under Master Arthur's very nose, so there was no getting a private inter-view with him. Secondly, Master Arthur himself, sitting on the ground with his terrier in his lap, directing the procee-dings by means of a donkey-headed stick with elaborately carved ears; and thirdly, Master Arthur's friend.

Now little bits of gossip will fly; and it had been heard in the dining-room, and conveyed by the parlour-maid to the kitchen, and passed from the kitchen into the village, that Master Arthur's friend was a very clever young gentleman; conse-quently Beauty Bill had been very anxious to see him. As, however, the clever young gentleman was lying on his back on the grass, with his hat flattened over his face to keep out the sun, and an open book lying on its face upon his waistcoat to keep the place, and otherwise quite immovable, and very like other young gentlemen, Bill did not feel much the wiser for looking at him. He had a better view of him soon, however, for Master Arthur began to poke his friend's legs with the donkey-headed stick, and to exhort him to get up.

"Hi! Bartram, get up! Here's my prime pupil. See what we can turn out. You may examine him if you like. Willie: this gentleman is a very clever gentleman, so you must keep your wits about you. *He'll* put questions to you, I can tell you! There's as much difference between his head and mine, as between mine and the head of this stick." And Master Arthur flourished his "one-legged donkey," as he called it, in the air, and added, "Bartram! you lazy lout! *will* you get up and take an interest in my humble efforts for the good of my fellow-creatures?"

Thus adjured, Mr. Bartram sat up with a jerk which threw his book on to his boots, and his hat after it, and looked at Bill. Now Bill and the gardener had both been grinning, as they always did at Master Arthur's funny speeches, but when Bill found the clever gentleman looking at him, he straightened his face very quickly. The gentleman was not at all like his friend ("nothing near so handsome," Bill reported at home), and he had such a large prominent forehead that he looked as if he were bald. When he sat up, he suddenly screwed up his eyes in a very peculiar way, pulled out a double gold eye-glass, fixed it on his nose, and stared through it for a second; after which his eyes unexpectedly opened to their full extent (they were not small ones), and took a sharp survey of Bill over the top of his spectacles; and this ended, he lay back on his elbow without speaking. Bill then and there decided that Mr. Bartram was very proud, rather mad, and the most disagreeable gentleman he ever saw; and he felt sure could see as well as he (Bill) could, and only wore spectacles out of a peculiar kind of pride and vain-glory which he could not exactly specify. Master Arthur seemed to think, at any rate, that he was not very civil, and began at once to talk to the boy himself.

"Why were you not at school last time, Willie? couldn't your mother spare you?"

"Yes, Sir."

"Then why didn't you come?" said Master Arthur, in evident astonishment.

Poor Bill! He stammered as he had stammered before the doctor, and finally gasped—

"Please, Sir, I was scared."

"Scared? What of?"

"Ghosts," murmured Bill in a very ghostly whisper. Mr. Bartram raised himself a little. Master Arthur seemed confounded.

"Why, you little goose! How is it you never were afraid before?"

"Please, Sir, I saw one the other night."

Mr. Bartram took another look over the top of his eye-glass and sat bolt upright, and John Gardener stayed his machine and listened, while poor Bill told the whole story of the Yew-lane Ghost.

When it was finished, the gardener, who was behind Master Arthur, said—

"I've heard something of this, Sir, in the village," and then added more which Bill could not hear.

"Eh, what?" said Master Arthur. "Willie, take the machine and drive about the garden a-bit wherever you like. Now, John."

Willie did not at all like being sent away at this interesting point. Another time he would have enjoyed driving over the short grass, and seeing it jump up like a little green fountain in front of him; but now his whole mind was absorbed by the few words he caught at intervals of the conversation going on between John and the young gentlemen. What could it mean? Mr. Bartram seemed to have awakened to extra-ordinary energy, and was talking rapidly. Bill heard the words "lime-light" and "large sheet," and thought they must be planning a magic-lantern exhibition, but was puzzled by catching the word "turnip." At last, as he was rounding the corner of a bed of geraniums, he distinctly heard Mr. Bartram ask—

"They cut the man's head off, didn't they?"

Then they were talking about the ghost, after all! Bill gave the machine a jerk, and to his dismay sliced a branch off one of the geraniums. What was to be done? He must tell Master Arthur, but he could not interrupt him just now; so on he drove, feeling very much dispirited, and by no means cheered by hearing shouts of laughter from the party on the grass. When one is puzzled and out of spirits, it is no consolation to hear other people laughing over a private joke; moreover, Bill felt that if they were still on the subject of the murdered man and his ghost, their merriment was very unsuitable. Whatever was going on, it was quite evident that Mr. Bartram was the leading spirit of it, for Bill could see Master Arthur waving the one legged donkey in an ecstasy, as he clapped his friend on the back till the eye-glass danced upon his nose. At last Mr. Bartram threw himself back as if closing a discussion, and said loud enough for Bill to hear—

"You never heard of a bully who wasn't a coward."

Bill thought of Bully Tom, and how he had said he dared not risk the chance of meeting with a ghost, and began to think that this was a clever young gentleman, after all. Just then Master Arthur called to him; and he took the bit of broken geranium and went.

"Oh, Willie!" said Master Arthur, "we've been talking over your misfortunes—geranium? fiddle-sticks! put it in your button-hole—your misfortunes, I say, and for to-night at any rate we intend to help you out of them. John—ahem!—will be—ahem!—engaged to-night, and unable to take his class as usual; but this gentleman has kindly consented to fill his place ("Hear, hear," said the gentleman alluded to), and if you'll come to-night, like a good lad, he and I will walk back with you; so if you do see the ghost, it will be in good company. But, mind, this is on one condition. You must not say anything about it—about our walking back with you, I mean—to anybody. Say nothing; but get ready and come to school as usual. You understand?"

"Yes, Sir," said Bill; "and I'm very much obliged to you, Sir, and the other gentleman as well."

Nothing more was said, so Bill made his best bow and retired. As he went he heard Master Arthur say to the gardener—

"Then you'll go to the town at once, John. We shall want the things as soon as possible. You'd better take the pony, and we'll have the list ready for you."

Juliana Horatia Ewing

Bill heard no more words; but as he left the grounds the laughter of the young gentlemen rang out into the road.

What did it all mean?

CHAPTER IV

"The night was now pitmirk; the wind soughed amid the headstones and railings of the gentry (for we all must die), and the black corbies in the steeple-holes cackled and crawed in a fearsome manner."

—MANSIE WAUGH

Bill was early at the night-school. No other of his class had arrived, so he took the corner by the fire sacred to first-comers, and watched the gradual gathering of the school. Presently Master Arthur appeared, and close behind him came his friend. Mr. Bartram Lindsay looked more attractive now than he had done in the garden. When standing, he was an elegant though plain-looking young man, neat in his dress, and with an admirable figure. He was apt to stand very still and silent for a length of time, and had a habit of holding his chin up in the air, which led some people to say that he "held himself very high." This was the opinion that Bill had formed, and he was rather alarmed by hearing Master Arthur pressing his friend to take his class instead of the more backward one, over which the gardener usually presided; and he was proportionably relieved when Mr. Bartram steadily declined.

"To say the truth, Bartram," said the young gentleman, "I am much obliged to you, for I am used to my own boys, and prefer them."

Then up came the schoolmaster.

"Mr. Lindsay going to take John's class? Thank you, Sir. I've put out the books; if you want anything else, Sir, p'raps you'll mention it. When they have done reading, perhaps, Sir, you will kindly draft them off for writing, and take the upper classes in arithmetic, if you don't object, Sir."

Mr. Lindsay did not object.

"If you have a picture or two," he said. "Thank you. Know their letters? All right. Different stages of progression. Very good. I've no doubt we shall get on together."

"Between ourselves, Bartram," whispered Master Arthur into his friend's ear, "the class is composed of boys who ought to have been to school, and haven't; or who have been, and are none the better for it. Some of them can what they call 'read in the Testament,' and all of them confound b and d when they meet with them. They are at one point of general information—namely, they all know what you have just told them, and will none of them know it by next time. I call it the rag-tag and bob-tail class. John says they are like forced tulips. They won't blossom simultaneously. He can't get them all to one standard of reading."

Mr. Lindsay laughed and said—

"He had better read less, and try a little general oral instruction. Perhaps they don't remember because they can't understand;"—and the Rector coming in at that moment, the business of the evening commenced.

Having afterwards to cross the school for something, Bill passed the new teacher and his class, and came to the conclusion that they did "get on together," and very well too. The rag-tag and bob-tail shone that night, and afterwards were loud in praises of the lesson. "It was so clear," and "He was so patient." Indeed, patience was one great secret of Mr. Lindsay's teaching; he waited so long for an answer that he generally got it. His pupils were obliged to exert themselves when there was no hope of being passed over, and everybody was waiting. Finally, Bill's share of the arithmetic lesson converted him to Master Arthur's friend. He *was* a clever young gentleman, and a kind one too.

The lesson had been so interesting—the clever young gentleman, standing (without his eye-glass) by the blackboard, had been so strict and yet so entertaining, was so obviously competent, and so pleasantly kind, that Bill, who liked arithmetic, and (like all intelligent children) appreciated good teaching, had had no time to think of the Yew-lane Ghost till the lesson was ended. It was not till the hymn began (they always ended the night-school with singing), then he remembered it. Then, while he was shouting with all his might Bishop Ken's glorious old lines—

"Keep me, oh keep me, King of kings,"

he caught Mr. Lindsay's eyes fixed on him, and back came the thoughts of his terrible fright, with a little shame too at his own timidity. Which of us trusts as we should do in the "defence of the Most High?"

Bill lingered as he had done the last time, and went out with the "grown-ups." It had been raining, and the ground was wet and sludgy, though it was fair overhead. The wind was cold, too, and Mr. Lindsay began to cough so violently, that Bill felt rather ashamed of taking him so far out of his way, through the damp chilly lane, and began to wonder whether he could not summon up courage to go alone. The result was, that with some effort he said—

"Please, Mr. Lindsay, Sir, I think you won't like to come so far this cold night. I'll try and manage, if you like."

Mr. Lindsay laid one hand on Bill's shoulder, and said quietly—

"No, thank you, my boy, we'll come with you, Thank you, all the same."

"Nevertheless, Bartram," said Master Arthur, "I wish you could keep that cough of yours quiet—it will spoil everything. A boy was eating peppermints in the shade of his copy-book this very night. I did box his ears; but I wish I had seized the goodies, they might have kept you quiet."

"Thank you," was the reply, "I abhor peppermint; but I have got some lozenges, if that will satisfy you. And when I smell ghosts, I can smother myself in my pocket-handkerchief."

Master Arthur laughed boisterously.

"We shall smell one if brimstone will do it. I hope he won't set himself on fire, or the scenic effect will be stronger than we bargained for."

This was the beginning of a desultory conversation carried on at intervals between the two young gentlemen, of which, though Bill heard every sentence, he couldn't understand one. He made one effort to discover what Master Arthur was alluding to, but with no satisfactory result, as we shall see.

"Please, Master Arthur," he said desperately, "you don't think there'll be two ghosts, do you, Sir?"

"I should say," said Master Arthur, so slowly and with such gravity that Bill felt sure he was making fun of him, "I should say, Bill, that if a place is haunted at all there is no limit to the number of ghosts—fifty quite as likely as one. What do you say, Bartram?"

"Quite so," said Bartram.

Bill made no further attempts to understand the mystery. He listened, but only grew more and more bewildered at the dark hints he heard, and never understood what it all meant until the end came; when (as is not uncommon) he wondered how he could have been so stupid, and why he had not seen it all from the very first.

They had now reached the turning-point, and as they passed into the dark lane, where the wind was shuddering and shivering among the trees, Bill shuddered and shivered too, and felt very glad that the young gentlemen were with him, after all.

Mr. Lindsay pulled out his watch.

"Well?" said his friend.

"Ten minutes to nine."

Then they walked on in silence, Master Arthur with one arm through his friend's, and the one-legged donkey under the other; and Mr. Lindsay with his hand on Bill's shoulder.

"I *should* like a pipe!" said Master Arthur presently; "it's so abominably damp."

"What a fellow you are," said Mr. Lindsay. "Out of the question! With the wind setting down the lane too! you talk of my cough—which is better, by-the-bye."

"What a fellow *you* are!" retorted the other. "Bartram, you are the oddest creature I know. What ever you take up, you do drive at so. Now I have hardly got a lark afloat before I'm sick of it. I wish you'd tell me two things—first, why are you so grave to-night? and, secondly, what made you take up our young friend's cause so warmly?"

"One answer will serve both questions," said Mr. Lindsay. "The truth is, old fellow, our young friend—[and Bill felt certain that the 'young friend' was himself]—has a look of a little chap I was chum with at school—Regy Gordon. I don't talk about it often, for I can't very well; but he was killed—think of it, man!—*killed* by such a piece of bullying as this! When they found him, he was quite stiff and speechless; he lived a few hours, but he only said two words—my name, and amen."

"Amen?" said Master Arthur, inquiringly.

"Well, you see when the surgeon said it was no go, they telegraphed for his friends; but they were a long way off, and he was sinking rapidly; and the old Doctor was in the room, half heart-broken, and he saw Gordon move his hands together, and he said, 'If any boy knows what prayers Gordon minor has been used to say, let him come and say them by him;' and I did. So I knelt by his bed and said them, the old Doctor kneeling too and sobbing like a child; and when I had done, Regy moved his lips and said 'Amen;' and then he said 'Lindsay!' and smiled, and then—"

Master Arthur squeezed his friend's arm tightly, but said nothing, and both the young men were silent; but Bill could not restrain his tears. It seemed the saddest story he had ever heard, and Mr. Lindsay's hand upon his shoulder shook so intolerably whilst he was speaking, that he had taken it away, which made Bill worse, and he fairly sobbed.

"What are you blubbering about, young 'un?" said Mr. Lindsay. "He is better off than any of us, and if you are a good boy you will see him some day;" and the young gentleman put his hand back again, which was steady now.

"What became of the other fellow?" said Master Arthur.

"He was taken away, of course. Sent abroad, I believe. It was hushed up. And now you know," added Mr. Lindsay, "why my native indolence has roused itself to get this cad taught a lesson, which many a time I wished to GOD when wishes were too late, that that other bully had been taught *in time*. But no one could thrash him; and no one durst complain. However, let's change the subject, old fellow! I've got over it long since: though sometimes I think the wish to see Regy again helps to keep me a decent sort of fellow. But when I saw the likeness this morning, it startled me; and then to hear the story, it seemed like a dream—the Gordon affair over again. I suppose rustic nerves are tougher; however, your village blackguard shan't have the chance of committing murder if we can cure him!"

"I believe you half wanted to undertake the cure yourself," said Master Arthur.

Mr. Lindsay laughed.

"I did for a minute. Fancy your father's feelings if I had come home with a black eye from an encounter with a pot-house bully! You know I put my foot into a tender secret of your man's, by offering to be the performer!"

"How?"

Mr. Lindsay lowered his voice, but not so that Bill could not hear what he said, and recognize the imitation of John Gardener.

"He said, 'I'd rather do it, if *you* please, Sir. The fact is, I'm partial to the young woman myself!' After that, I could but leave John to defend his young woman's belongings."

"Gently!" exclaimed Master Arthur. "There is the Yew Walk."

From this moment the conversation was carried on in whispers, to Bill's further mystification. The young gentlemen recovered their spirits, and kept exploding in smothered chuckles of laughter.

"Cold work for him if he's been waiting long!" whispered one.

"Don't know. His head's under cover, remember!" said the other: and they laughed.

"Bet you sixpence he's been smearing his hand with brimstone for the last half hour."

"Don't smell him yet, though."

"He'll be a patent aphis-destroyer in the rose-garden for months to come."

"Sharp work for the eyelids if it gets under the sheet."

They were now close by the Yews, out of which the wind came with a peculiar chill, as if it had been passing through a vault. Mr. Bartram Lindsay stooped down, and whispered in Bill's ear. "Listen, my lad. We can't go down the lane with you, for we want to see the ghost, but we don't want the ghost to see us. Don't be frightened, but go just as usual. And mind—when you see the white figure, point with your own arm *towards the Church*, and scream as loud as you like. Can you do this?"

"Yes, Sir," whispered Bill.

"Then off with you. We shall creep quietly on behind the trees; and you shan't be hurt, I promise you."

Bill summoned his courage, and plunged into the shadows. What could be the meaning of Mr. Lindsay's strange orders? Should he ever have courage to lift his arm towards the church in the face of that awful apparition of the murdered man? And if he did, would the unquiet spirit take the hint, and go back into the grave, which Bill knew was at that very corner to which he must point? Left alone, his terrors began to return; and he listened eagerly to see if, amid the ceaseless soughing of the wind among the long yew branches, he could hear the rustle of the young men's footsteps as they crept behind. But he could distinguish nothing. The hish-wishing of the thin leaves was so incessant, the wind was so dexterous and tormenting in the tricks it played and the sounds it produced, that the whole place seemed alive with phantom rustlings and footsteps; and Bill felt as if Master Arthur was right, and that there was "no limit" to the number of ghosts!

At last he could see the end of the avenue. There among the few last trees was the place where the ghost had appeared. There beyond lay the white road, the churchyard corner, and the tall grey tomb-stone glimmering in the moonlight. A few steps more, and slowly from among the yews came the ghost as before, and raised its long white arm. Bill determined that, if he died for it, he would do as he had been told; and lifting his own hand he pointed towards the tomb-stone, and gave a shout. As he pointed, the ghost turned round, and then— rising from behind the tomb-stone, and gliding slowly to the edge of the wall, which separated the churchyard from the lower level of the road—there appeared a sight so awful, that Bill's shout merged into a prolonged scream of terror.

Truly Master Arthur's anticipations of a "scenic effect" were amply realized. The walls and buttresses of the old Church stood out dark against the sky; the white clouds sailed slowly by the moon, which reflected itself on the damp grass, and shone upon the flat wet tomb-stones till they looked like pieces of water. It was not less bright upon the upright ones, upon quaint crosses, short headstones, and upon the huge ungainly memorial of the murdered Ephraim Garnett. But *the* sight on which it shone that night was the figure now standing by Ephraim Garnett's grave, and looking over the wall. An awful figure, of gigantic height, with ghostly white garments clinging round its headless body, and carrying under its left arm the head that should have been upon its shoulders. On this there was neither flesh nor hair. It seemed to be a bare skull, with fire gleaming through the hollow eye-sockets and the grinning teeth. The right hand of the figure was outstretched as if in warning; and from the palms to the tips of the fingers was a mass of lambent flame. When Bill saw this fearful apparition he screamed with hearty good will; but the noise he made was nothing to the yell of terror that came from beneath the shroud of the Yew-lane Ghost, who, on catching sight of the rival spectre, fled wildly up the lane, kicking the white sheet off as he went, and finally displaying, to Bill's amazement, the form and features of Bully Tom. But this was not all. No sooner had the first ghost started, than the second (not to be behind-hand) jumped nimbly over the wall, and gave chase. But fear had put wings on to Bully Tom's feet; and the second ghost being somewhat encumbered by his costume, judged it wisdom to stop; and then taking the fiery skull in its flaming hands, shied it with such dexterity, that it hit Bully Tom in the middle of his back, and falling on to the wet ground, went out with a hiss. This blow was an unexpected shock to the Bully, who thought the ghost must have come up to him with supernatural rapidity, and falling on his knees in the mud, began to roar most lustily:

"Lord, have mercy upon me! I'll never do it no more!"

Mr. Lindsay was not likely to alter his opinion on the subject of bullies. This one, like others, was a mortal coward. Like other men, who have no fear of GOD before their eyes, he made up for it by having a very hearty fear of sickness, death, departed souls, and one or two other things, which the most self-willed sinner knows well enough to be in the hands of a Power which he cannot see, and does not wish to believe in. Bully Tom had spoken the truth when he said that if he thought there was a ghost in Yew-lane he wouldn't go near it. If he had believed the stories with which he had alarmed poor Bill, the lad's evening walk would never have been disturbed, as far as he was concerned. Nothing but his spite against Bessy would have made him take so much trouble to vex the peace, and stop the schooling, of her pet brother; and as it was, the standing alone by the churchyard at night was a position so little to his taste, that he had drunk pretty heavily in the public-house for half an hour beforehand, to keep up his spirits. And now he had been paid back in his own coin, and lay grovelling in the mud, and calling profanely on the Lord, Whose mercy such men always cry for in their trouble, if they never ask it for their sins. He was so confused and blinded by drink and fright, that he did not see the second ghost divest himself of his encumbrances, or know that it was John Gardener, till that rosy-cheeked worthy, his clenched hands still flaming with brimstone, danced round him, and shouted scornfully, and with that vehemence of aspiration, in which he was apt to indulge when excited:

"Get hup, yer great cowardly booby, will yer? So you thought you was coming hout to frighten a little lad, did ye? And you met with one of your hown size, did ye? Now *will* ye get hup and take it like a man, or shall I give it you as ye lie there?"

Juliana Horatia Ewing

Bully Tom chose the least of two evils, and staggering to his feet with an oath, rushed upon John. But in his present condition he was no match for the active little gardener, inspired with just wrath, and thoughts of Bessy; and he then and there received such a sound thrashing as he had not known since he first arrogated the character of village bully. He was roaring loudly for mercy, and John Gardener was giving him a harmless roll in the mud by way of conclusion, when he caught sight of the two young gentlemen in the lane—Master Arthur in fits of laughter at the absurd position of the ex-Yew-lane Ghost and Mr. Lindsay standing still and silent, with folded arms, set lips, and the gold eye-glass on his nose. As soon as he saw them, he began to shout, "Murder! help!" at the top of his voice.

"I see myself," said Master Arthur, driving his hands contemptuously into his pockets—"I see myself helping a great lout who came out to frighten a child, and can neither defend his own eyes and nose, nor take a licking with a good grace when he deserves it!"

Bully Tom appealed to Mr. Lindsay.

"Yah! yah!" he howled: "will you see a man killed for want of help?"

But the clever young gentleman seemed even less inclined to give his assistance.

"Killed!" he said contemptuously; "I *have* seen a lad killed on such a night as this, by such a piece of bullying! Be thankful you have been stopped in time! I wouldn't raise my little finger to save you from twice such a thrashing. It has been fairly earned! Give the ghost his shroud, Gardener, and let him go; and recommend him not to haunt Yew-lane in future."

John did so, with a few words of parting advice on his own account.

"Be hoff with you," he said. "Master Lindsay, he speaks like a book. You're a disgrace to your hage and sect, you are! I'd as soon fight with an old charwoman. Though, bless you, young gentlemen," he added, as Bully Tom slunk off muttering, "he *is* the biggest blackguard in the place; and what the Rector'll say, when he comes to know as you've been mingled up with him, passes me."

"He'll forgive us, I dare say," said Master Arthur. "I only wish he could have seen you emerge from behind that stone! It was a sight for a century! I wonder what the youngster thought of it! Hi, Willie, here, Sir! What did you think of the second ghost?"

Bill had some doubts as to the light in which he ought to regard that apparition; but he decided on the simple truth.

"I thought it looked very horrid, Sir."

"I should hope it did! The afternoon's work of three able-bodied men has been marvellously wasted if it didn't. However, I must say you halloed out loud enough!"

Bill coloured, the more so as Mr. Lindsay was looking hard at him over the top of his spectacles.

"Don't you feel rather ashamed of all your fright, now you've seen the ghosts without their sheets?" inquired the clever young gentleman.

"Yes, Sir," said Bill, hanging his head. "I shall never believe in ghosts again, Sir, though."

Mr. Bartram Lindsay took off his glasses, and twiddled them in his fingers.

"Well, well," he said in a low hurried voice; "I'm not the parson, and I don't pretend to say what you should believe and what you shouldn't. We know precious little as to how much the spirits of the dead see and know of what they have left behind. But I think you may venture to assure yourself that when a poor soul has passed the waves of this troublesome world, by whatever means, it doesn't come back kicking about under a white sheet in dark lanes, to frighten little boys from going to school."

"And that's very true, Sir," said John Gardener, admiringly.

"So it is," said Master Arthur. "I couldn't have explained that myself, Willie; but those are my sentiments and I beg you'll attend to what Mr. Lindsay has told you."

"Yes, Sir," said Bill.

Mr. Lindsay laughed, though not quite merrily, and said—

"I could tell him something more, Arthur, though he's too young to understand it: namely, that if he lives, the day will come, when he would be only too happy if the dead might come back and hold out their hands to us, anywhere, and for however short a time."

The young gentleman stopped abruptly; and the gardener heaved a sympathetic sigh.

"I tell you what it is, Bartram," muttered Master Arthur, "I suppose I'm too young, too, for I've had quite enough of the melancholies for one night. As to you, you're as old as the hills; but it's time you came home; and if I'd known before what you told me to night, old fellow, you shouldn't have come out on this expedition. Now, for you, Willie," added the young gentleman, whirling sharply round, "if you're not a pattern Solomon henceforth, it won't be the fault of your friends. And if wisdom doesn't bring you to school after this, I shall try the argument of the one-legged donkey."

"I don't think I shall miss next time, Sir."

"I hope you won't. Now, John, as you've come so far, you may as well see the lad safe home; but don't shake hands with the family in the present state of your fists, or you might throw somebody into a fit. Good-night!"

Yew-lane echoed a round of "Good-nights;" and Bill and the gardener went off in high spirits. As they crossed the road, Bill looked round, and under the trees saw the young gentlemen strolling back to the Rectory, arm in arm. Mr. Bartram Lindsay with his chin high in the air, and Master Arthur vehemently exhorting him on some topic, of which he was pointing the moral with flourishes of the one-legged donkey.

* * * * *

For those who like to know "what became of" everybody, these facts are added:

The young gentlemen got safely home; and Master Arthur gave such a comical account of their adventure, that the Rector laughed too much to scold them, even if he had wished.

Beauty Bill went up and down Yew-lane on many a moonlight night after this one, but he never saw another ghost, or felt any more fears in connection with Ephraim

Juliana Horatia Ewing

Garnett. To make matters more entirely comfortable, however, John kindly took to the custom of walking home with the lad after night-school was ended. In return for this attention, Bill's family were apt to ask him in for an hour; and by their fire-side he told the story of the two ghosts so often—from the manufacture in the Rectory barn to the final apparition at the cross-roads—that the whole family declare they feel just as if they had seen it.

Bessy, under the hands of the cheerful doctor, got quite well, and eventually married. As her cottage boasts the finest window plants in the village, it is shrewdly surmised that her husband is a gardener.

Bully Tom talked very loudly for some time of "having the law of" the rival ghost; but finding, perhaps, that the story did not redound to his credit, was unwilling to give it further publicity, and changed his mind.

Winter and summer, day and night, sunshine and moonlight, have passed over the lane and the churchyard, and the wind has had many a ghostly howl among the yews, since poor Bill learnt the story of the murder; but he knows now that the true Ephraim Garnett has never been seen on the cross-roads since a hundred years ago, and will not be till the Great Day.

In the ditch by the side of Yew-lane shortly after the events I have been describing, a little lad found a large turnip, in which someone had cut eyes, nose, and mouth, and put bits of stick for teeth. The turnip was hollow, and inside it was fixed a bit of wax candle. He lighted it up, and the effect was so splendid, that he made a show of it to his companions at the price of a marble each, who were well satisfied. And this was the last of the Yew-lane Ghosts.

A BAD HABIT

CHAPTER I

"Oh, how much more doth beauty beauteous seem
By that sweet ornament which truth doth give!
The rose looks fair, but fairer we it deem
For that sweet odour which doth in it live."

—SHAKESPEARE

My godmother, Lady Elizabeth, used to say, "Most things are matters of habit. Good habits and bad habits." And she generally added, "*Your* bad habit, Selina, is a habit of grumbling."

I was always accustomed to seeing great respect paid to anything my godmother said or did. In the first place, she was what Mrs. Arthur James Johnson called "a fine lady," and what the maids called "a real lady." She was an old friend and, I think, a relative of my father, who had married a little below his own rank—my mother being the daughter of a rich manufacturer. My father had died before I can remember things, and Joseph and I lived with our mother and her friends. At least, we were with our mother when she could bear the noise; and for the rest of our time, when we were tired of playing games together, we sat with the maids.

"That is where you learned your little *toss* and your trick of grumbling, my dear," my godmother said, planting her gold eye-glasses on her high nose; "and that is why your mouth is growing out of shape, and your forehead getting puckered, and your chin poked, and—and your boots bulged crooked."

"*My boots*, godmother?"

"Your boots, my dear. No boots will keep in shape if you shake your hips and kick with your heels like a servant out Sunday walking. When little girls flounce on the high road, it only looks ridiculous; but when you grow up, you'll never have a clean petticoat, or be known for a well-bred woman behind your back, unless you learn to walk as if your legs and your feelings were under your own control. That is why the sergeant is coming to-morrow and every week-day morning to drill you and Joseph from ten to eleven whilst you remain here."

And my godmother pressed the leaves of the journal on her lap, and cut them quite straight and very decisively with a heavy ivory paper-knife.

I had never been taught that it is bad manners to mutter—nurse always talked to herself when she was "put out"—and, as I stood in much awe of Lady Elizabeth, I did not like to complain aloud of her arrangements. So I turned my doll with a sharp flounce in my arms, and muttered behind her tarlatan skirts that "I did think we were to have had whole holidays out visiting."

I believe my godmother heard me; but she only looked at me

for a moment over the top of her gold eye-glasses, and then went on reading the paper through them.

After a few moments, she laid it down on her lap with her left hand, and with her right hand took off her eye-glasses and held them between her fingers.

"I shall be sorry if you don't grow up nice-looking, Selina," she said. "It's a great advantage to a woman—indeed, to anyone—to be good-looking. Your mother was a pretty woman, too; and your father—"

Lady Elizabeth stopped, and then, seeming suddenly to see that I was watching her and waiting, put her glasses before her eyes again, and continued—

"Your father was a very good-looking gentleman, with a fine face and a fine figure, beautiful eyes and mouth, very attractive hands, and most fascinating manners. It will be a pity if you don't grow up nice-looking."

I grew crimson, partly with mortification and partly with astonishment. I had a strong natural desire to be pretty, but I felt sure I had been taught somehow that it was much more meritorious not to care about it. It certainly did not please me when (if I had offended them) the maids said I should never be as pretty as Maud Mary Ibbetson, my bosom friend; but when nurse took the good looking-glass out of the nursery, and hung up the wavy one which used to be in her room instead, to keep me from growing vain, I did not dispute her statement that "the less little girls looked in the glass the better." And when I went to see Maud Mary (who was the only child of rich parents, and had a cheval-glass in her own bed-room), it was a just satisfaction to me to feel that if she was prettier, and could see herself full length, she was probably vainer than I.

It was very mortifying, therefore, to find that my godmother not only thought me plain, but gave me no credit for not minding it. I grew redder and redder, and my eyes filled with tears.

Lady Elizabeth was very nice in one way—she treated us with as much courtesy and consideration as if we were grown up. People do not think about being polite to children, but my godmother was very polite.

"My dear child," she said, holding out her hand, "I am very sorry if I have hurt your feelings. I beg your pardon."

I put my hot and rather dirty little paw among her cool fingers and diamond rings. I could not mutter to her face, but I said rather under my sobs that "it seemed such a thing" to be blamed for not being pretty.

"My dear Selina, I never said anything about your being pretty. I said I should be sorry if you did not grow up nice-looking, which is quite another thing. It will depend on yourself whether you are nice-looking or not."

I began to feel comforted, but I bridled my chin in an aggrieved manner, which I know I had caught from Mrs. Marsden, the charwoman, when she took tea in the nursery and told long tales to nurse; and I said I "was sure it wasn't for want of speaking to" nurse that my hair did not wave like Maud Mary's, but that when I asked her to crimp it, she only said, "Handsome is that handsome does, and that ought to be enough for you, Miss Selina, without *my* slaving to damp-plait your hair every night."

I repeated nurse's speech pretty volubly, and with her sharp accent and accompanying toss. My godmother heard me out, and then she said—

"Nurse quoted a very good proverb, which is even truer than it is allowed to be. Those who do well grow to look well. My little goddaughter, that soft child's face of yours can be pinched and pulled into a nice shape or an ugly shape, very much as you pull and pinch that gutta-percha head I gave you, and, one way or another, it is being shaped all along."

"But people can't give themselves beautiful figures, and eyes, and mouths, and hands, as you said papa had, unless they are born so," I objected.

"Your father's figure, my dear," said Lady Elizabeth, "was beautiful with the grace and power which comes of training. He was a military man, and you have only to look at a dozen common men in a marching regiment and compare them with a dozen of the same class of men who go on plodding to work and loafing at play in their native villages, to see what people can do for their own figures. His eyes, Selina, were bright with intelligence and trained powers of observation; and they were beautiful with kindliness, and with the well-bred habit of giving complete attention to other people and their affairs when he talked with them. He had a rare smile, which you may not inherit, but the real beauty of such mouths as his comes from the lips being restrained into firm and sensitive lines, through years of self-control and fine sympathies."

I do not quite understand. "Do you mean that I can practise my mouth into a nice shape?" I asked.

"Certainly not, my dear, any more than you can pinch your nose into shape with your finger and thumb; but your lips, and all the lines of your face, will take shape of themselves, according to your temper and habits.

"There are two things," my godmother continued, after

Juliana Horatia Ewing

turning round to look at me for a minute, "there are two things, Selina, against your growing up good-looking. One is that you have caught so many little vulgarisms from the servants; and the other is your little bad habit of grumbling, which, for that matter, is a very ill-bred habit as well, and would spoil the prettiest eyes, nose, mouth, and chin that ever were inherited. Under-bred and ill-educated women are, as a general rule, much less good-looking than well-bred and highly-educated ones, especially in middle life; not because good features and pretty complexions belong to one class more than to another, but because nicer personal habits and stricter discipline of the mind do. A girl who was never taught to brush her teeth, to breathe through the nostrils instead of the lips, and to chew with the back teeth instead of the front, has a very poor chance of growing up with a pretty mouth, as anyone may see who has observed a middle-aged woman of that class munching a meat pie at a railway-station. And if, into the bargain, she has nothing to talk about but her own and her neighbour's everyday affairs, and nothing to think about to keep her from continually talking, life, my dear child, is so full of little rubs, that constant chatter of this kind must almost certainly be constant grumbling. And constant grumbling, Selina, makes an ugly under-lip, a forehead wrinkled with frowning, and dull eyes that see nothing but grievances. There is a book in the library with some pictures of faces that I must show you. Do you draw at all, my dear?"

"Mamma gave me a drawing-slate on my birthday," I replied, "but Joseph bothered me to lend it to him, and now he's broken the glass. It *is* so tiresome! But it's always the way if you lend things."

"What makes you think that it is always the way if you lend things?" my godmother gently inquired.

"It seems as if it was, I'm sure," was my answer. "It was just the same with the fish-kettle when cook lent it to the Browns. They kept it a fortnight, and let it rust, and the first time cook put a drop of water into it it leaked; and she said it always *was* the way; you might lend everything you had, and people had no conscience, but if it came to borrowing a pepperpot—"

My godmother put up both her long hands with an impatient gesture.

"That will do, my dear. I don't care to hear all that your mother's cook said about the fish-kettle."

I felt uncomfortable, and was glad that Lady Elizabeth went on talking.

"Have you and Joseph any collections? When I was your age, I remember I made a nice collection of wafers. They were quite as pretty as modern monograms."

"Joseph collected feathers out of the pillows once," I said, laughing. "He got a great many different sorts, but nurse burned them, and he cried."

"I'm sorry nurse burned them. I daresay they made him very happy. I advise you to begin a collection, Selina. It is a capital cure for discontent. Anything will do. A collection of buttons, for instance. There are a great many kinds; and if ever some travelled friend crowns your collection with a mandarin's button, for one day at least you won't feel a grievance worth speaking of."

I was feeling very much aggrieved as Lady Elizabeth spoke, and thinking to myself that "it seemed so hard to be scolded out visiting, and when one had not got into any scrape." But I only said that "nobody at home ever said that I grumbled so much;" and that I "didn't know that our servants complained more than other people's."

"I do not suppose they do," said my godmother. "I have told you already that I consider it a foible of ill-educated people, whose interests are very limited, and whose feelings are not disciplined. You know James, the butler, Selina, do you not?"

"Oh, yes, godmamma!"

I knew James well. He was very kind to me, and always liberal when, by Lady Elizabeth's orders, he helped me to almonds and raisins at dessert.

"My mother died young," said Lady Elizabeth, "and at sixteen I was head of my father's household. I had been well trained, and I tried to do my duty. Amid all the details of providing for and entertaining many people, my duty was to think of everything, and never to seem as if I had anything on my mind. I should have been fairly trained *for a kitchen-maid*, Selina, if I had done what I was told when it was bawled at me, and had talked and seemed more over-whelmed with work than the Prime Minister. Well, most of our servants had known me from babyhood, and it was not a light matter to have the needful authority over them without hurting the feelings of such old and faithful friends. But, on the whole, they respected my efforts, and were proud of my self-possession. I had more trouble with the younger ones, who were too young to help me, and whom I was too young to overawe. I was busy one morning writing necessary letters, when James—who was then seventeen, and the under-footman—came to the drawing room and wished to speak to me. When he had wasted a good deal of my time in describing his unwillingness to disturb me, and the years his father had lived in my father's service, I said, 'James, I have important letters to write, and very little time to spare. If you have any complaint to make, will you kindly put it as shortly as you can?' 'I'm sure, my lady, I have no wish to complain,' was James's reply; and thereon his complaints poured forth in a continuous stream. I took out my watch (unseen by James, for I never insult people), and gave him five minutes for his grievances. He got on pretty fast with them. He had mentioned the stone floor of his bed-room, a draught in the pantry, the overbearingness of the butler, the potatoes for the servants' hall being under-boiled when the cook was out of temper, the inferior quality of the new plate-powder, the insinuations against his father's honesty by servants who were upstarts by comparison, his hat having been spoilt by the rain, and that he never was so miserable in his life—when the five minutes expired, and I said 'Then, James, you want to go?' He coloured, and I really think tears stood in his eyes. He was a good-hearted lad.

"When he began to say that he could never regard any other place as he looked on this, and that he felt towards his lordship and me as he could feel towards no other master and mistress, I gave him another five minutes for what he was pleased with. To do him justice, the list was quite as long as that of his grievances. No people were like us, and he had never been so happy in his life. So I said, 'Then, James, you want to stay?'

"James began a fresh statement, in which his grievances and his satisfactions came alternately, and I cut this short by saying, 'Well, James, the difficulty seems to be that you have not made up your mind what you do want. I have no time to balance matters for you, so you had better go downstairs and think it well over, and let me know what you decide.'"

"He went accordingly, and when he was driven to think for

himself by being stopped from talking to me, I suppose he was wise enough to perceive that it is easier to find crosses in one's lot than to feel quite sure that one could change it for a better. I have no doubt that he had *not* got all he might lawfully have wished for, but, different as our positions were, no more had I, and we both had to do our duty and make the best of life as we found it. It's a very good thing, dear child, to get into the habit of saying to oneself, 'One can't have everything.' I suppose James learned to say it, for he has lived with me ever since."

At this moment Joseph called to me through the open window which led into the garden—

"Oh, Selina! I am so sorry; but when I got to the shop I couldn't remember whether it was a quarter of a yard of ribbon or three-quarters that you wanted for the doll's hat."

Joseph was always doing stupid things like this. It vexed me very much, and I jumped up and hastily seized my doll to go out and speak to him, saying, as I did so, that "boys were enough to drive one wild, and one might as well ask the poodle to do anything as Joseph." And it was not till I had flounced out of the drawing-room that I felt rather hot and uncomfortable to remember that I had tossed my head, and knitted my brows, and jerked my chin, and pouted my lips, and shaken my skirts, and kicked up my heels, as I did so, and that my godmother had probably been observing me through her gold eye-glasses.

CHAPTER II

"It is easier to prevent ill habits than to break them."

—OLD PROVERB

I must say that Joseph *was* rather a stupid boy. He was only a year younger than me, but I never could make him understand exactly what I wanted him to do when we played together; and he was always saying, "Oh, I say, look here, Selina!" and proposing some silly plan of his own. But he was very good-natured, and when we were alone I let him be uncle to the dolls. When we spent the day with Maud Mary, however, we never let him play with the baby-house; but we allowed him to be the postman and the baker, and people of that sort, who knock and ring, and we sent him messages.

During the first week of our visit to Lady Elizabeth, the weather was so fine that Joseph and I played all day long in the garden. Then it became rainy, and we quarrelled over the old swing and the imperfect backgammon board in the lumber-room, where we were allowed to amuse ourselves. But one morning when we went to our play-room, after drilling with Sergeant Walker, Joseph found a model fortress and wooden soldiers and cannon in one corner of the room; and I found a Dutch market, with all kinds of wooden booths, and little tables to have tea at in another. They were presents from my godmother; and they were far the best kind of toys we had ever had, you could do so many things with them.

Joseph was so happy with his soldiers that he never came near the Dutch fair; and at other times he was always bothering to be allowed to play with the dolls. At first I was

Juliana Horatia Ewing

very glad, for I was afraid he would be coming and saying, "Oh, I say, Selina," and suggesting things; and I wanted to arrange the shops my own way. But when they were done, and I was taking the dolls from one booth to another to shop, I did think it seemed very odd that Joseph should not even want to walk through the fair. And when I gave him leave to be a shopkeeper, and to stand in front of each booth in turn, he did not seem at all anxious to come; and he would bring a cannon with him, and hide it behind his back when I came to buy vegetables for the dolls' dinners.

We quarrelled about the cannon. I said no one ever heard of a greengrocer with a cannon in his shop; and Joseph said it couldn't matter if the greengrocer stood in front of the cannon so as to hide it. So I said I wouldn't have a cannon in my fair at all; and Joseph said he didn't want to come to my fair, for he liked his fortress much better, and he rattled out, dragging his cannon behind him, and knocked down Adelaide Augusta, the gutta-percha doll, who was leaning against the fishmonger's slab, with her chin on the salmon.

It was very hard, and I said so; and then Joseph said there were plenty of times when I wouldn't let him play with the dolls; and I said that was just it—when I didn't want him to he wanted, and when I wanted him to he wouldn't, and that he was very selfish.

So at last he put away his cannon, and came and played at shops; but he was very stupid, and would look over his shoulder at the fortress when he ought to have been pretending to sell; and once, when I had left the fair, he got his cannon back and shot peas out of it, so that all the fowls fell off the real hooks in the poulterer's shop, and said he was bombarding the city.

I was very angry, and said, "I shall go straight down, and

complain to godmamma," and I went.

The worst of it was that only that very morning Lady Elizabeth had said to me, "Remember one thing, my dear. I will listen to no complaints whatever. No grumbles either from you or from Joseph. If you want anything that you have not got, and will ask for it, I will do my best for you, as my little guests; and if it is right and reasonable, and fair to both, you shall have what you want. But you must know your own mind when you ask, and make the best of what I can do for you. I will hear no general complaints whatever."

Remembering this, I felt a little nervous when I was fairly in the drawing-room, and Lady Elizabeth had laid down her glasses to hear what I had to say.

"Do you want anything, my dear?" said she.

I began to complain—that Joseph was so stupid; that it seemed so provoking; that I did think it was very unkind of him, etc.; but Lady Elizabeth put up her hand.

"My dear Selina, you have forgotten what I told you. If there is anything that an old woman like me can do to make your father's child happy, do not be afraid to ask for it, but I will not have grumbling in the drawing-room. By all means make up your mind as to what you want, and don't be afraid to ask your old godmother. But if she thinks it right to refuse, or you do not think it right to ask, you must make the best of matters as they stand, and keep your good humour and your good manners like a lady."

I felt puzzled. When I complained to nurse that Joseph "was so tiresome," she grumbled back again that "she never knew such children," and so forth. It is always easy to meet grievance with grievance, but I found that it was not so easy

Juliana Horatia Ewing

to make up my mind and pluck up my courage to ask in so many words for what I wanted.

"Shall I ask Joseph to put away his cannon and come and play at your game for an hour now, my dear? I will certainly forbid him to fire into your shop."

This did not quite satisfy me. As a matter of fact, Joseph had left his fortress to play with me; and I did not really think he would discharge his cannon at the poulterer's again. But I thought myself hardly used, and I wanted my godmother to think so too, and to scold Joseph. What else I wanted, I did not feel quite sure.

"I wish you would speak to Joseph," I said. "He would attend to you if you told him how selfish and stupid he is."

"My dear, I never offered to complain to Joseph, but I will order him not to molest you, and I will ask him to play with you."

"I'm sure I don't want him to play with me, unless he can play nicely, and invent things for the dolls to say, as Maud Mary would," was my reply; for I was getting thoroughly vexed.

"Then I will tell him that unless he can play your game as you wish it, he had better amuse himself with his own toys. Is there anything else that you want, my dear?"

I could not speak, for I was crying, but I sobbed out that "I missed Maud Mary so."

"Who is Maud Mary, Selina?"

"Maud Mary Ibbetson, my particular friend—my *very*

particular friend," I explained.

I spoke warmly, for at that moment the memory of Maud Mary seemed adorable, and I longed to pour my complaints into her sympathetic ear. Besides, I had another reason for regretting that she was not with me. When we were together, it was she, as a rule, who had new and handsome toys to exhibit, whilst I played the humbler part of admirer. But if she had been with me, then, what would not have been my triumph in displaying the Dutch fair! The longer I thought of her the faster my tears fell, but they did not help me to think of anything definite to ask for; and when Lady Elizabeth said, "would you like to go home, my dear? or do you want me to ask your friend to stay with you?" I had the grace to feel ashamed of my peevishness, and to thank my godmother for her kindness, and to protest against wanting anything more. I only added, amid my subsiding sobs, that "it did seem such a thing," when I had got a Dutch fair to play at dolls in, that Joseph should be so stupid, and that dear Maud Mary, who would have enjoyed it so much, should not be able to see it.

Juliana Horatia Ewing

CHAPTER III

"Nous aurons aussi la fete dans notre rue."

—RUSSIAN PROVERB

Next day, when our drill in the long corridor was over, Lady Elizabeth told Joseph to bring his fortress, guns, and soldiers into the library, and to play at the Thirty Years' War in the bay-window from a large book with pictures of sieges and battles, which she lent him.

To me my godmother turned very kindly and said, "I have invited your little friend Maud to come and stay here for a week. I hope she will arrive to-day, so you had better prepare your dolls and your shops for company."

Maud Mary coming! I danced for joy, and kissed my godmother, and expressed my delight again and again. I should have liked to talk about it to Joseph, but he had plunged into the Thirty Years' War, and had no attention to give me.

It was a custom in the neighbourhood where my mother lived to call people by double Christian names, John Thomas, William Edward, and so forth; but my godmother never called Maud Mary anything but Maud.

It was possible that my darling friend might arrive by the twelve o'clock train, and the carriage was sent to meet her, whilst I danced up and down the big hall with impatience. When it came back without her my disappointment knew no bounds. I felt sure that the Ibbetsons' coachman had been unpunctual, or dear Maud Mary's nurse had been cross, as usual, and had not tried to get her things packed. I rushed into the library full of my forebodings, but my godmother only said, "No grumbling, my dear!" and Joseph called out, "Oh, I say, Selina, I wish you wouldn't swing the doors so: you've knocked down Wallenstein, and he's fallen on the top of Gustavus Adolphus;" and I had to compose myself as best I could till the five o'clock train.

Then she came. Darling Maud Mary!

Perhaps it was because I crushed her new feather in kissing her (and Maud Mary was very particular about her clothes); perhaps it was because she was tired with travelling, which I forgot; or perhaps it was because she would rather have had tea first, that Maud Mary was not quite so nice about the Dutch fair as I should have liked her to be.

She said she rather wondered that Lady Elizabeth had not given me a big dolls' house like hers instead; that she had come away in such a hurry that she forgot to lock hers up, and she should not be the least surprised if the kitten got into it and broke something, but "it did seem rather odd" to be invited in such a very hurried way; that just when she *was* going to a big house to pay a grand visit, of course the dressmaker "disappointed" Mrs. Ibbetson, but "that was the way things always did happen;" that the last time Mr. Ibbetson was in Paris he offered to bring her a dolls' railway train, with real first-class carriages really stuffed, but she said she would rather have a locket, and that was the very one which was hanging round her neck, and which was much handsomer than Lucy Jane Smith's, which cost five pounds in London.

Maud Mary's inattention to the fair and the dolls was so obvious that I followed my godmother's advice, and "made the best of it" by saying, "I'm afraid you're very much tired, darling?"

Maud Mary tossed her chin and frowned.

It was "enough to tire anybody," she said, to travel on that particular line. The railway of which her papa was a director was very differently managed.

I think my godmother's courtesy to us, and her thoughtful kindness, had fixed her repeated hints about self-control and good manners rather firmly in my head. I distinctly remember making an effort to forget my toys and think of Maud Mary's comfort.

I said, "Will you come and take off your things, darling?" and she said, "Yes, darling;" and then we had tea.

But next day, when she was quite rested, and had really nothing to complain of, I did think she might have praised the Dutch fair.

She said it "seemed such a funny thing" to have to play in an old garret; but she need not have wanted to alter the arrangement of all the shops, and have everything her own way, as she always had at home, because, if her dolls' house was hers, my Dutch fair was mine. I did think, for a moment, of getting my godmother to speak to her, but I knew it would be of no use to complain unless I had something to ask for. When I came to think of it, I found that what I wanted was that Maud Mary should let me manage my own toys and direct the game, and I resolved to ask her myself.

"Look here, darling," said I, "when I come and play with you, I always play dolls as you like, because the dolls' house is yours; I wish you would play my game to-day, as the Dutch fair is mine."

Maud Mary flounced to her feet, and bridled with her wavy head, and said she was sure she did not want to play if I didn't like her way of playing; and as to my Dutch fair, her papa could buy her one any day for her very own.

I was nettled, for Maud Mary was a little apt to flourish Mr. Ibbetson's money in my face; but if her father was rich, my godmother was a lady of rank, and I said that "my godmother, Lady Elizabeth, said it was very vulgar to flounce and toss one's head if one was put out."

Maud Mary crimsoned, and, exclaiming that she did not care what Lady Elizabeth or Lady Anybody Else said, she whisked over three shops with the ends of her sash, and kicked the wax off Josephine Esmeralda's nose with the heel of her Balmoral boot.

I don't like confessing it, but I did push Maud Mary, and Maud Mary slapped me.

And when we both looked up, my godmother was standing before us, with her gold spectacles on her nose.

*　　*　　*　　*　　*

Lady Elizabeth was very kind, and even then I knew that she was very right.

When she said, "I have asked your friend for a week, and for that week, my dear, she is your guest, and you must try to please, and *make the best of it*," I not only did not dispute it; I felt a spirit of self-suppression and hospitable pride awake within me to do as she had said.

I think the hardest part of it was that, whatever I did and whatever I gave up, Maud Mary recognized no effort on my part. What she got she took as her due, and what she did not get she grumbled about.

I sometimes think that it was partly because, in all that long week, she never ceased grumbling, that I did; I hope for life.

Only once I said, "O godmamma! how glad I shall be when I am alone with Joseph again!" And with sudden remorse, I added, "But I beg your pardon, that's grumbling; and you *have* been so kind!"

Lady Elizabeth took off her eye-glasses, and held out her hands for mine.

"Is it grumbling, little woman?" she said. "Well, I'm not sure."

"*I'm* not sure," I said, smiling; "for you know I only said I should be so *glad* to be alone with Joseph, and to try to be good to him; for he is a very kind boy, and if he is a little awkward with the dolls, I mean to make the best of it. *One can't have everything*," I added, laughing.

Lady Elizabeth drew my head towards her, and stroked and kissed it.

"GOD bless you, child," she said. "You *have* inherited your father's smile."

* * * * *

"But, I say, Selina," whispered Joseph, when I went to look at his fortress in the bay-window. "Do you suppose it's because he's dead that she cried behind her spectacles when she said you had got his smile?"

A HAPPY FAMILY

CHAPTER I

"If solid happiness we prize,
Within our breast this jewel lies.

    *   *   *   *   *

From our own selves our joys must flow,
And peace begins at home."

—COTTON

The family—our family, not the Happy Family—consisted of me and my brothers and sisters. I have a father and mother, of course.

I am the eldest, as I remind my brothers; and of the more worthy gender, which my sisters sometimes forget. Though we live in the village, my father is a gentleman, as I shall be when I am grown up. I have told the village boys so more than once. One feels mean in boasting that one is better born than they are; but if I did not tell them, I am not sure that they would always know.

Juliana Horatia Ewing

Our house is old, and we have a ghost—the ghost of my great-great-great-great-great-aunt.

She "crossed her father's will," nurse says, and he threatened to flog her with his dog-whip, and she ran away, and was never heard of more. He would not let the pond be dragged, but he never went near it again; and the villagers do not like to go near it now. They say you may meet her there, after sunset, flying along the path among the trees, with her hair half down, and a knot of ribbon fluttering from it, and parted lips, and terror in her eyes.

The men of our family (my father's family, my mother is Irish) have always had strong wills. I have a strong will myself.

People say I am like the picture of my great-grandfather (the great-great-great-nephew of the ghost). He must have been a wonderful old gentleman by all accounts. Sometimes nurse says to us, "Have your own way, and you'll live the longer," and it always makes me think of great-grandfather, who had so much of his own way, and lived to be nearly a hundred.

I remember my father telling us how his sisters had to visit their old granny for months at a time, and how he shut the shutters at three o'clock on summer afternoons, and made them play dummy whist by candle light.

"Didn't you and your brothers go?" asked Uncle Patrick, across the dinner-table. My father laughed.

"Not we! My mother got us there once—but never again."

"And did your sisters like it?"

"Like it? They used to cry their hearts out. I really believe it killed poor Jane. She was consumptive and chilly, but always craving for fresh air; and granny never would have open windows, for fear of draughts on his bald head; and yet the girls had no fires in their room, because young people shouldn't be pampered."

"And ye never-r offer-r-ed—neither of ye—to go in the stead of them?"

When Uncle Patrick rolls his R's in a discussion, my mother becomes nervous.

"One can't expect boys to consider things," she said. "Boys will be boys, you know."

"And what would you have 'em be?" said my father. Uncle Patrick turned to my mother.

"Too true, Geraldine. Ye don't expect it. Worse luck! I assure ye, I'd be aghast at the brutes we men can be, if I wasn't more amazed that we're as good as we are, when the best and gentlest of your sex—the moulders of our childhood, the desire of our manhood—demand so little for all that you alone can give. There were conceivable uses in women preferring the biggest brutes of barbarous times, but it's not so now; and boys will be civilised boys, and men will be civilised men, sweet sister, when you *do* expect it, and when your grace and favours are the rewards of nobleness, and not the easy prize of selfishness and savagery."

My father spoke fairly.

"There's some truth in what you say, Pat."

"And small grace in my saying it. Forgive me, John."

That's the way Uncle Patrick flares up and cools down, like a straw bonfire. But my father makes allowances for him; first, because he is an Irishman, and, secondly, because he's a cripple.

* * * * *

I love my mother dearly, and I can do anything I like with her. I always could. When I was a baby, I would not go to sleep unless she walked about with me, so (though walking was bad for her) I got my own way, and had it afterwards.

With one exception. She would never tell me about my godfather. I asked once, and she was so distressed that I was glad to promise never to speak of him again. But I only thought of him the more, though all I knew about him was his portrait—such a fine fellow—and that he had the same swaggering, ridiculous name as mine.

How my father allowed me to be christened Bayard I cannot imagine. But I was rather proud of it at one time—in the days when I wore long curls, and was so accustomed to hearing myself called "a perfect picture," and to having my little sayings quoted by my mother and her friends, that it made me miserable if grown-up people took the liberty of attending to anything but me. I remember wriggling myself off my mother's knee when I wanted change, and how she gave me her watch to keep me quiet, and stroked my curls, and called me her fair-haired knight, and her little Bayard; though, remembering also, how lingeringly I used just not to do her bidding, ate the sugar when she wasn't looking, tried to bawl myself into fits, kicked the nurse-girl's shins, and dared not go upstairs by myself after dark—I must confess that a young chimpanzee would have as good claims as I had to represent that model of self-conquest and true chivalry, "the Knight without fear and without reproach."

However, the vanity of it did not last long. I wonder if that grand-faced godfather of mine suffered as I suffered when he went to school and said his name was Bayard? I owe a day in harvest to the young wag who turned it into Backyard. I gave in my name as Backyard to every subsequent inquirer, and Backyard I modestly remained.

Juliana Horatia Ewing

CHAPTER II

"The lady with the gay macaw."

—LONGFELLOW

My sisters are much like other fellows' sisters, excepting Lettice. That child is like no one but herself.

I used to tease the other girls for fun, but I teased Lettice on principle—to knock the nonsense out of her. She was only eight, and very small, but, from the top row of her tight little curls to the rosettes on her best shoes, she seemed to me a mass of affectation.

Strangers always liked Lettice. I believe she was born with a company voice in her mouth; and she would flit like a butterfly from one grown-up person to another, chit-chattering, whilst some of us stood pounding our knuckles in our pockets, and tying our legs into knots, as we wished the drawing-room carpet would open and let us through into the cellar to play at catacombs.

That was how Cocky came. Lettice's airs and graces bewitched the old lady who called in the yellow chariot, and was so like a cockatoo herself—a cockatoo in a citron velvet bonnet, with a bird of Paradise feather. When that old lady put up her eye-glass, she would have frightened a yard-dog; but Lettice stood on tip-toes and stroked the feather, saying, "What a love-e-ly bird!" And next day came Cocky—perch and all complete—*for the little girl who loves birds*. Lettice was proud of Cocky, but Edward really loved him, and took trouble with him.

Edward is a good boy. My mother called him after the Black Prince.

He and I disgraced ourselves in the eyes of the Cockatoo lady, and it cost the family thirty thousand pounds, which we can ill afford to lose. It was unlucky that she came to luncheon the very day that Edward and I had settled to dress up as Early Britons, in blue woad, and dine off earth-nuts in the shrubbery. As we slipped out at the side door, the yellow chariot drove up to the front. We had doormats on, as well as powder-blue, but the old lady was terribly shocked, and drove straight away, and did not return. Nurse says she is my father's godmother, and has thirty thousand pounds, which she would have bequeathed to us if we had not offended her. I take the blame entirely, because I always made the others play as I pleased.

We used to play at all kinds of things—concerts, circuses, theatricals, and sometimes conjuring. Uncle Patrick had not been to see us for a long time, when one day we heard that he was coming, and I made up my mind at once that I would have a perfectly new entertainment for him.

We like having entertainments for Uncle Patrick, because he is such a very good audience. He laughs, and cries, and claps, and thumps with his crutch, and if things go badly, he amuses the rest.

Ever since I can remember anything, I remember an old print, called "The Happy Family," over our nursery fire-place, and how I used to wonder at that immovable cat, with sparrows on her back, sitting between an owl and a magpie. And it was when I saw Edward sitting with Benjamin the cat, and two sparrows he had brought up by hand, struggling and laughing because Cocky would push itself, crest first, under his waistcoat, and come out at the top to kiss him—that an idea struck me; and I resolved to have a Happy Family for Uncle Patrick, and to act Showman myself.

Edward can do anything with beasts. He was absolutely necessary as confederate, but it was possible Lettice might want to show off with Cocky, and I did not want a girl on the stage, so I said very little to her. But I told Edward to have in the yard-dog, and practise him in being happy with the rest of the family pets. Fred, the farm-boy, promised to look out for an owl. Benjamin, the cat, could have got mice enough; but he would have eaten them before Edward had had time to teach him better, so I set a trap. I knew a village-boy with a magpie, ready tamed.

Bernard, the yard-dog, is a lumbering old fellow, with no tricks. We have tried. We took him out once, into a snow-drift, with a lantern round his neck, but he rescued nothing, and lost the lantern—and then he lost himself, for it was dark.

But he is very handsome and good, and I knew, if I put him in the middle, he would let anything sit upon him. He would not feel it, or mind if he did. He takes no notice of Cocky.

Benjamin never quarrels with Cocky, but he dare not forget that Cocky is there. And Cocky sometimes looks at Benjamin's yellow eyes as if it were thinking how very easily they would come out. But they are quite sufficiently happy together for a Happy Family.

The mice gave more trouble than all the rest, so I settled that Lettice should wind up the mechanical mouse, and run that on as the curtain rose.

CHAPTER III

"Memor esto majorum."

—OLD MOTTO

" . . . .All my fears are laid aside,
If I but remember only
Such as these have lived and died!"

—LONGFELLOW

Do you wish to avoid vexations? Then never have a Happy Family! Mine were countless.

Fred could not get me an owl. Lettice *did* want to show off with Cocky. I had my own way, but she looked sulky and spiteful. I got Tom Smith's magpie; but I had to have him, too. However, my costume as Showman was gorgeous, and Edward kept our Happy Family well together. We arranged that Tom should put Mag on at the left wing, and then run round behind, and call Mag softly from the right. Then she would hop across the stage to him, and show off well. Lettice was to let mother know when the spectators might take their places, and to tell the gardener when to raise the curtain.

I really think one magpie must be "a sign of sorrow," as nurse says; but what made Bernard take it into his beautiful foolish head to give trouble I cannot imagine. He wouldn't lie down, and when he did, it was with a *grump* of protest that seemed to forbode failure. However, he let Cocky scold him and pull his hair, which was a safety-valve for Cocky. Benjamin dozed with dignity. He knew Cocky wasn't watching for his yellow eyes.

I don't think Lettice meant mischief when she summoned the spectators, for time was up. But her warning the curtain to rise when it did was simple malice and revenge.

I never can forget the catastrophe, but I do not clearly remember how Tom Smith and I *began* to quarrel. He was excessively impudent, and seemed to think we couldn't have had a Happy Family without him and his chattering senseless magpie.

When I told him to remember he was speaking to a gentleman, he grinned at me.

"A gentleman? Nay, my sakes! Ye're not civil enough by half. More like a new policeman, if ye weren't such a Guy Fawkes in that finery."

"Be off," said I, "and take your bird with you."

"What if I won't go?"

"I'll make you!"

"Ye darsen't touch me."

"Daren't I?"

"Ye darsen't."

"I dare."

"Try."

"*Are* you going?"

"Noa."

I only pushed him. He struck first. He's bigger than me, but he's a bigger coward, and I'd got him down in the middle of the stage, and had given him something to bawl about, before I became conscious that the curtain was up. I only realised it then, because civil, stupid Fred, arrived at the left wing, panting and gasping—

"Measter Bayard! Here's a young wood-owl for ye."

As he spoke, it escaped him, fluff and feathers flying in the effort, and squawking, plunging, and fluttering, made wildly for the darkest corner of the stage, just as Lettice ran on the mechanical mouse in front.

Bernard rose, and shook off everything, and Cocky went into screaming hysterics; above which I now heard the thud of Uncle Patrick's crutch, and the peals upon peals of laughter with which our audience greeted my long-planned spectacle of a Happy Family!

*　*　*　*　*

Our Irish uncle is not always nice. He teases and mocks, and has an uncertain temper. But one goes to him in trouble. I went next morning to pour out my woes, and defend myself, and complain of the others.

I spoke seriously about Lettice. It is not pleasant for a fellow to have a sister who grows up peculiar, as I believe Lettice will. Only the Sunday before, I told her she would be just the sort of woman men hate, and she said she didn't care; and I said she ought to, for women were made for men, and the Bible says so; and she said grandmamma said that every soul was made for GOD and its own final good. She was in a high-falutin mood, and said she wished she had been christened Joan instead of Lettice, and that I would be a true

Bayard; and that we could ride about the world together, dressed in armour, and fighting for the right. And she would say all through the list of her favourite heroines, and asked me if I minded *their* being peculiar, and I said of course not, why should you mind what women do who don't belong to you? So she said she could not see that; and I said that was because girls can't see reason; and so we quarrelled, and I gave her a regular lecture, which I repeated to Uncle Patrick.

He listened quite quietly till my mother came in, and got fidgetty, and told me not to argue with my uncle. Then he said—

"Ah! let the boy talk, Geraldine, and let me hear what he has to say for himself. There's a sublime audacity about his notions, I tell ye. Upon me conscience, I believe he thinks his grandmother was created for his particular convenience."

That's how he mocks, and I suppose he meant my Irish grandmother. He thinks there's nobody like her in the wide world, and my father says she is the handsomest and wittiest old lady in the British Isles. But I did not mind. I said,

"Well, Uncle Patrick, you're a man, and I believe you agree with me, though you mock me."

"Agree with ye?" He started up, and pegged about the room. "Faith! if the life we live is like the globe we inhabit—if it revolves on its own axis, *and you're that axis*—there's not a flaw in your philosophy; but IF—Now perish my impetuosity! I've frightened your dear mother away. May I ask, by the bye, if *she* has the good fortune to please ye, since the Maker of all souls made her, for all eternity, with the particular object of mothering you in this brief patch of time?"

He had stopped under the portrait—my godfather's portrait. All his Irish rhodomontade went straight out of my head, and I ran to him.

"Uncle, you know I adore her! But there's one thing she won't do, and, oh, I wish you would! It's years since she told me never to ask, and I've been on honour, and I've never even asked nurse; but I don't think it's wrong to ask you. Who is that man behind you, who looks such a wonderfully fine fellow? My Godfather Bayard."

I had experienced a shock the night before, but nothing to the shock of seeing Uncle Patrick's face then, and hearing him sob out his words, instead of their flowing like a stream.

"Is it possible? Ye don't know? She can't speak of him yet? Poor Geraldine!"

He controlled himself, and turned to the picture, leaning on his crutch. I stood by him and gazed too, and I do not think, to save my life, I could have helped asking—

"Who is he?"

"Your uncle. Our only brother. Oh, Bayard, Bayard!"

"Is he dead?"

He nodded, speechless; but somehow I could not forbear.

"What did he die of?"

"Of unselfishness. He died—for others."

"Then he *was* a hero? That's what he looks like. I am glad he is my godfather. Dear Uncle Pat, do tell me all about it."

"Not now—hereafter. Nephew, any man—with the heart of man and not of a mouse—is more likely than not to behave well at a pinch; but no man who is habitually selfish can be *sure* that he will, when the choice comes sharp between his own life and the lives of others. The impulse of a supreme moment only focusses the habits and customs of a man's soul. The supreme moment may never come, but habits and customs mould us from the cradle to the grave. His were early disciplined by our dear mother, and he bettered her teaching. Strong for the weak, wise for the foolish—tender for the hard—gracious for the surly—good for the evil. Oh, my brother, without fear and without reproach! Speak across the grave, and tell your sister's son that vice and cowardice become alike impossible to a man who has never—cradled in selfishness, and made callous by custom—learned to pamper himself at the expense of others!"

I waited a little before I asked—

"Were you with him when he died?"

"I was."

"Poor Uncle Patrick! What *did* you do?"

He pegged away to the sofa, and threw himself on it.

"Played the fool. Broke an arm and a thigh, and damaged my spine, and—*lived*. Here rest the mortal remains."

And for the next ten minutes, he mocked himself, as he only can.

* * * * *

One does not like to be outdone by an uncle, even by such an uncle; but it is not very easy to learn to live like Godfather Bayard.

Sometimes I wish my grandmother had not brought up her sons to such a very high pitch, and sometimes I wish my mother had let that unlucky name become extinct in the family, or that I might adopt my nickname. One could live up to *Backyard* easily enough. It seems to suit being grumpy and tyrannical, and seeing no further than one's own nose, so well.

But I do try to learn unselfishness; though I sometimes think it would be quite as easy for the owl to learn to respect the independence of a mouse, or a cat to be forbearing with a sparrow!

I certainly get on better with the others than I used to do; and I have some hopes that even my father's godmother is not finally estranged through my fault.

Uncle Patrick went to call on her whilst he was with us. She is very fond of "that amusing Irishman with the crutch," as she calls him; and my father says he'll swear Uncle Patrick entertained her mightily with my unlucky entertainment, and that she was as pleased as Punch that her cockatoo was in the thick of it.

I am afraid it is too true; and the idea made me so hot, that if I had known she was really coming to call on us again, I should certainly have kept out of the way. But when Uncle Patrick said, "If the yellow chariot rolls this way again, Bayard, ye need not be pursuing these archaeological revivals of yours in a too early English costume," I thought it was only his chaff. But she did come.

I was pegging out the new gardens for the little ones. We

were all there, and when she turned her eye over us (just like a cockatoo), and said, in a company voice—

"What a happy little family!"

I could hardly keep my countenance, and I heard Edward choking in Benjamin's fur, where he had hidden his face.

But Lettice never moved a muscle. She clasped her hands, and put her head on one side, and said—in *her* company voice—"But you know brother Bayard *is* so good to us now, and *that* is why we are such A HAPPY FAMILY."

* * * * *

Choose from Thousands of 1stWorldLibrary Classics By

A. M. Barnard
Ada Leverson
Adolphus William Ward
Aesop
Agatha Christie
Alexander Aaronsohn
Alexander Kielland
Alexandre Dumas
Alfred Gatty
Alfred Ollivant
Alice Duer Miller
Alice Turner Curtis
Alice Dunbar
Allen Chapman
Alleyne Ireland
Ambrose Bierce
Amelia E. Barr
Amory H. Bradford
Andrew Lang
Andrew McFarland Davis
Andy Adams
Angela Brazil
Anna Alice Chapin
Anna Sewell
Annie Besant
Annie Hamilton Donnell
Annie Payson Call
Annie Roe Carr
Annonaymous
Anton Chekhov
Archibald Lee Fletcher
Arnold Bennett
Arthur C. Benson
Arthur Conan Doyle
Arthur M. Winfield
Arthur Ransome
Arthur Schnitzler
Arthur Train
Atticus
B.H. Baden-Powell
B. M. Bower
B. C. Chatterjee
Baroness Emmuska Orczy
Baroness Orczy
Basil King
Bayard Taylor
Ben Macomber
Bertha Muzzy Bower
Bjornstjerne Bjornson

Booth Tarkington
Boyd Cable
Bram Stoker
C. Collodi
C. E. Orr
C. M. Ingleby
Carolyn Wells
Catherine Parr Traill
Charles A. Eastman
Charles Amory Beach
Charles Dickens
Charles Dudley Warner
Charles Farrar Browne
Charles Ives
Charles Kingsley
Charles Klein
Charles Hanson Towne
Charles Lathrop Pack
Charles Romyn Dake
Charles Whibley
Charles Willing Beale
Charlotte M. Braeme
Charlotte M. Yonge
Charlotte Perkins Stetson
Clair W. Hayes
Clarence Day Jr.
Clarence E. Mulford
Clemence Housman
Confucius
Coningsby Dawson
Cornelis DeWitt Wilcox
Cyril Burleigh
D. H. Lawrence
Daniel Defoe
David Garnett
Dinah Craik
Don Carlos Janes
Donald Keyhoe
Dorothy Kilner
Dougan Clark
Douglas Fairbanks
E. Nesbit
E. P. Roe
E. Phillips Oppenheim
E. S. Brooks
Earl Barnes
Edgar Rice Burroughs
Edith Van Dyne
Edith Wharton

Edward Everett Hale
Edward J. O'Biren
Edward S. Ellis
Edwin L. Arnold
Eleanor Atkins
Eleanor Hallowell Abbott
Eliot Gregory
Elizabeth Gaskell
Elizabeth McCracken
Elizabeth Von Arnim
Ellem Key
Emerson Hough
Emilie F. Carlen
Emily Bronte
Emily Dickinson
Enid Bagnold
Enilor Macartney Lane
Erasmus W. Jones
Ernie Howard Pie
Ethel May Dell
Ethel Turner
Ethel Watts Mumford
Eugene Sue
Eugenie Foa
Eugene Wood
Eustace Hale Ball
Evelyn Everett-green
Everard Cotes
F. H. Cheley
F. J. Cross
F. Marion Crawford
Fannie E. Newberry
Federick Austin Ogg
Ferdinand Ossendowski
Fergus Hume
Florence A. Kilpatrick
Fremont B. Deering
Francis Bacon
Francis Darwin
Frances Hodgson Burnett
Frances Parkinson Keyes
Frank Gee Patchin
Frank Harris
Frank Jewett Mather
Frank L. Packard
Frank V. Webster
Frederic Stewart Isham
Frederick Trevor Hill
Frederick Winslow Taylor

Friedrich Kerst
Friedrich Nietzsche
Fyodor Dostoyevsky
G.A. Henty
G.K. Chesterton
Gabrielle E. Jackson
Garrett P. Serviss
Gaston Leroux
George A. Warren
George Ade
Geroge Bernard Shaw
George Cary Eggleston
George Durston
George Ebers
George Eliot
George Gissing
George MacDonald
George Meredith
George Orwell
George Sylvester Viereck
George Tucker
George W. Cable
George Wharton James
Gertrude Atherton
Gordon Casserly
Grace E. King
Grace Gallatin
Grace Greenwood
Grant Allen
Guillermo A. Sherwell
Gulielma Zollinger
Gustav Flaubert
H. A. Cody
H. B. Irving
H.C. Bailey
H. G. Wells
H. H. Munro
H. Irving Hancock
H. R. Naylor
H. Rider Haggard
H. W. C. Davis
Haldeman Julius
Hall Caine
Hamilton Wright Mabie
Hans Christian Andersen
Harold Avery
Harold McGrath
Harriet Beecher Stowe
Harry Castlemon
Harry Coghill
Harry Houidini

Hayden Carruth
Helent Hunt Jackson
Helen Nicolay
Hendrik Conscience
Hendy David Thoreau
Henri Barbusse
Henrik Ibsen
Henry Adams
Henry Ford
Henry Frost
Henry James
Henry Jones Ford
Henry Seton Merriman
Henry W Longfellow
Herbert A. Giles
Herbert Carter
Herbert N. Casson
Herman Hesse
Hildegard G. Frey
Homer
Honore De Balzac
Horace B. Day
Horace Walpole
Horatio Alger Jr.
Howard Pyle
Howard R. Garis
Hugh Lofting
Hugh Walpole
Humphry Ward
Ian Maclaren
Inez Haynes Gillmore
Irving Bacheller
Isabel Cecilia Williams
Isabel Hornibrook
Israel Abrahams
Ivan Turgenev
J.G.Austin
J. Henri Fabre
J. M. Barrie
J. M. Walsh
J. Macdonald Oxley
J. R. Miller
J. S. Fletcher
J. S. Knowles
J. Storer Clouston
J. W. Duffield
Jack London
Jacob Abbott
James Allen
James Andrews
James Baldwin

James Branch Cabell
James DeMille
James Joyce
James Lane Allen
James Lane Allen
James Oliver Curwood
James Oppenheim
James Otis
James R. Driscoll
Jane Abbott
Jane Austen
Jane L. Stewart
Janet Aldridge
Jens Peter Jacobsen
Jerome K. Jerome
Jessie Graham Flower
John Buchan
John Burroughs
John Cournos
John F. Kennedy
John Gay
John Glasworthy
John Habberton
John Joy Bell
John Kendrick Bangs
John Milton
John Philip Sousa
John Taintor Foote
Jonas Lauritz Idemil Lie
Jonathan Swift
Joseph A. Altsheler
Joseph Carey
Joseph Conrad
Joseph E. Badger Jr
Joseph Hergesheimer
Joseph Jacobs
Jules Vernes
Julian Hawthrone
Julie A Lippmann
Justin Huntly McCarthy
Kakuzo Okakura
Karle Wilson Baker
Kate Chopin
Kenneth Grahame
Kenneth McGaffey
Kate Langley Bosher
Kate Langley Bosher
Katherine Cecil Thurston
Katherine Stokes
L. A. Abbot
L. T. Meade

L. Frank Baum
Latta Griswold
Laura Dent Crane
Laura Lee Hope
Laurence Housman
Lawrence Beasley
Leo Tolstoy
Leonid Andreyev
Lewis Carroll
Lewis Sperry Chafer
Lilian Bell
Lloyd Osbourne
Louis Hughes
Louis Joseph Vance
Louis Tracy
Louisa May Alcott
Lucy Fitch Perkins
Lucy Maud Montgomery
Luther Benson
Lydia Miller Middleton
Lyndon Orr
M. Corvus
M. H. Adams
Margaret E. Sangster
Margret Howth
Margaret Vandercook
Margaret W. Hungerford
Margret Penrose
Maria Edgeworth
Maria Thompson Daviess
Mariano Azuela
Marion Polk Angellotti
Mark Overton
Mark Twain
Mary Austin
Mary Catherine Crowley
Mary Cole
Mary Hastings Bradley
Mary Roberts Rinehart
Mary Rowlandson
M. Wollstonecraft Shelley
Maud Lindsay
Max Beerbohm
Myra Kelly
Nathaniel Hawthrone
Nicolo Machiavelli
O. F. Walton
Oscar Wilde

Owen Johnson
P.G. Wodehouse
Paul and Mabel Thorne
Paul G. Tomlinson
Paul Severing
Percy Brebner
Percy Keese Fitzhugh
Peter B. Kyne
Plato
Quincy Allen
R. Derby Holmes
R. L. Stevenson
R. S. Ball
Rabindranath Tagore
Rahul Alvares
Ralph Bonehill
Ralph Henry Barbour
Ralph Victor
Ralph Waldo Emmerson
Rene Descartes
Ray Cummings
Rex Beach
Rex E. Beach
Richard Harding Davis
Richard Jefferies
Richard Le Gallienne
Robert Barr
Robert Frost
Robert Gordon Anderson
Robert L. Drake
Robert Lansing
Robert Lynd
Robert Michael Ballantyne
Robert W. Chambers
Rosa Nouchette Carey
Rudyard Kipling
Saint Augustine
Samuel B. Allison
Samuel Hopkins Adams
Sarah Bernhardt
Sarah C. Hallowell
Selma Lagerlof
Sherwood Anderson
Sigmund Freud
Standish O'Grady
Stanley Weyman
Stella Benson
Stella M. Francis

Stephen Crane
Stewart Edward White
Stijn Streuvels
Swami Abhedananda
Swami Parmananda
T. S. Ackland
T. S. Arthur
The Princess Der Ling
Thomas A. Janvier
Thomas A Kempis
Thomas Anderton
Thomas Bailey Aldrich
Thomas Bulfinch
Thomas De Quincey
Thomas Dixon
Thomas H. Huxley
Thomas Hardy
Thomas More
Thornton W. Burgess
U. S. Grant
Upton Sinclair
Valentine Williams
Various Authors
Vaughan Kester
Victor Appleton
Victor G. Durham
Victoria Cross
Virginia Woolf
Wadsworth Camp
Walter Camp
Walter Scott
Washington Irving
Wilbur Lawton
Wilkie Collins
Willa Cather
Willard F. Baker
William Dean Howells
William le Queux
W. Makepeace Thackeray
William W. Walter
William Shakespeare
Winston Churchill
Yei Theodora Ozaki
Yogi Ramacharaka
Young E. Allison
Zane Grey